Healing Voices

From Behind The Chair

Aundrea Booker along with 11 other empowering women

© 2024 All Rights Reserved

HerEmpire Media Publishing

All rights reserved. No part of this publication may be reproduced, distributed, or transmitted in any form or by any means, including photocopying, recording, or other electronic or mechanical methods, without the prior written permission of the publisher, except in the case of brief quotations embodied in critical reviews and certain other non commercial uses permitted by copyright law.

This book is a work of nonfiction. The information presented herein represents the views of the authors as of the date of publication. It is sold with the understanding that the publisher is not engaged in rendering legal, accounting, or other professional services. If legal advice or other expert assistance is required, the services of a competent professional should be sought.

Table of Contents

INTRODUCTION: ……………………………………......5

How I Found Healing And Purpose Through My Business
By Aundrea Booker …………………………………….……6

My Life Beyond The Chair
By Nina Moorer …………………………………….....….14

Phenomenally Blessed
By Kiara Allen ……………………………………….....21

The Goddess and the Dragon: Unleashing My Sacred Power
By Choya Woods ……………………………………....27

Lost in the Nightlife: Finding Myself Again
By Aleisha Kuntu ………………………………………...42

The Forever Student: Finding Peace in Endless Learning
By Yolanda Long …………………………………….....49

The Crown We Wear: A Story of Self-Love and Resilience
By Monèl Antut …………………………………..…......56

My Testimony: My Portrait
By Kiauna Montgomery ………………………………..65

From Paralysis To Progress A Star Is Born
By Sherronda Booker ……………………………….....69

Reclaiming Your Strength and Wholeness
By Kathy Rivers ……………………………………..…………………..82

Cutting Through Life
By Vernee Nycole ………………………………………..……....90

Overcoming Darkness and Finding My Light
By Regina McClarn ……………………………………..……….100

What's Your Next Step? ……………………………………...106

INTRODUCTION:

Healing Voices From Behind The Chair

In a world often focused on appearances, the beauty industry stands out as a realm where transformation goes beyond the surface. *Healing Voices: From Behind The Chair* brings together twelve remarkable women who have dedicated their lives to enhancing not only beauty but also the emotional well-being of those they touch. Each author in this anthology has honed her craft and developed a unique approach to physical transformation, but their stories extend far beyond their professional expertise.

In these pages, you will find powerful narratives that reveal the personal battles each woman has faced—challenges that have shaped their identities and deepened their strength and purpose. As they share their journeys of resilience, they invite you to witness the intersections of struggle and success, vulnerability and strength. These stories highlight the transformative power of connection, reminding us that true healing often occurs when we open ourselves to others and share our stories.

Aundrea Booker

CEO & Founder Tre-Azure LLC

www.Tre-Azure.com
https://www.facebook.com/aundrea.booker
https://www.instagram.com/mssatin2silk/

Aundrea Booker is a powerhouse in the beauty industry, with over 23 years of expertise as a hairstylist and the visionary CEO and founder of Tre-Azure LLC, a groundbreaking line of healthy hair tools and products designed for multi-textured hair. As the proud co-owner of Simple Cuts Plus Hair Salon, a multicultural, family-oriented salon, Aundrea has built a reputation for delivering personalized hair care that enhances her clients' natural beauty.

Her salon is a welcoming, inclusive space where clients leave feeling confident, beautiful, and educated about their hair. Aundrea's mission is clear: to empower others by helping them embrace their confidence, starting with healthy hair. Through her work behind the chair and her innovative product line, Aundrea is redefining beauty and transforming lives, one client at a time.

How I Found Healing And Purpose Through My Business

By: Aundrea Booker

It was a cold January morning in 2022 when my phone rang, and I had no idea what impact that call would have. It was a life-changing call. My world came crashing down. I didn't know if I was coming or going. To this day, I'm still living with some of the effects of that year. Even thinking about it right now to write this makes my heart beat fast.

It was the beginning of the year, and I remember being woken up by this call. The person on the phone said my grandson's dad had gotten shot and that he was no longer alive. I wondered why my daughter hadn't called and discovered she didn't know yet. That made my anxiety even worse. Anticipating the phone call from her was so scary for me.

And then the moment that I had been dreading came. She called.

"Mom," she said, her voice cracking. "He's gone."

The sound of her sobs ripped through the phone and my heart; I could hardly breathe. I wasn't ready for this.

"How do I tell him, Mom? How do I tell my son his father isn't coming back?"

The sadness in her voice. The tears in her voice. I couldn't have prepared myself for it. She was so worried about telling her son, my grandson, what had happened. And I was just as confused as she was. I felt like I was powerless and of no help to her.

In those dark moments, we leaned on God more than ever. As a family, we would come together each night and pray for strength and understanding.

"Jehovah, I don't know why this is happening," I prayed several nights, with tears streaming down my face. "But we need you to help us through."

Through the grace of God, prayer, and family loving on each other, we actually started to navigate through this tough time over the next few months. I thought that was one of the worst feelings I could've ever encountered. I struggled through it. We struggled through it together.

Might I remind you, at this time, my other daughter, the eldest, was pregnant, and this was very difficult for her as well.

Months slipped by in a haze of grief, and before I knew it, August arrived. My other daughter was now preparing to bring new life into the world. For a moment, we thought this baby girl would be a light in our darkness. But life, once again, had other plans. We were so excited to welcome this beautiful baby girl into our family.

Unfortunately, the happiness was short-lived for all of us, especially my daughter, who had just given birth. Like déjà vu, I got a phone call the next morning after the birth that her older son's dad had been stabbed and didn't make it.

If you're anything like me, I know you are thinking, what in the world is going on? This couldn't be happening. I was in such disbelief. It was another gut punch. Once again, I was lost and didn't know how to help my children. I didn't know how to help my grandchildren. I had never experienced anything like this because my dad is still alive, and both of my parents are.

When this happened, it had a triggering effect on my other daughter. All the work she had done came crashing down because it was like reliving her loss all over again—to see her sister and nephew go through the same thing she and her son had just struggled through. Although you never really get over death, you just kinda learn how to live with it. With all that was happening, I couldn't have prepared myself for what would happen next.

I had a regular work day, came home, and grabbed my beautiful 11-day-old granddaughter from my daughter. We began our usual routine of me beginning to play with her. Today, something seemed off. I asked my daughter why she was not responding as usual. She replied, "She hadn't eaten today and hadn't been herself." After a couple more minutes of looking at her, I advised my daughter to take her to urgent care so they could check her out and ensure she was OK.

She got her all dressed up and bundled up and took her to the urgent care. An hour or so later, I received a call from her saying that they would take her to the emergency room because they were also concerned. They wanted to keep her for observation because she was so little, which I totally understood.

A couple of hours after they arrived at the hospital, I received another kind of disturbing call. It was from my daughter. She said it was not looking good and didn't think she would make it. I was totally shocked because nothing seemed that detrimental when they left. I thought my daughter was overreacting. I was very concerned, so I got dressed and headed to the hospital very quickly.

While en route, the nurse called to explain what was happening. I was still quite confused. None of this made sense to me. I figured I would see what was going on when I arrived.

When I arrived, as I stepped into the hospital room, the beeping of machines and whispered voices of doctors filled the air. My daughter stood there, pale and motionless, her face a ghostly shadow of the joy she had felt just days ago. I felt the room spinning, and a lump lodged in my throat. Her eyes met mine, and it was like the world stopped for a second.

Long story short, from when she arrived at the urgent care until I arrived at the hospital, it had been about 11 hours. All I remember is that the doctors said they were gonna take her off the ventilator. There was no more they could do. They prepared the room and gave us time to say our last goodbyes. Without going into too many graphic details, it was the saddest thing I've ever endured in my life.

As a mother and grandmother, I did not know what to do once again. I did not know how to help.

You always wanna rescue your children, your grandchildren and shield them from life's pains. But I was helpless. I couldn't do anything. Having to come home and explain to my grandson that his sister had just passed away 11 days after his dad passed away was unbearable.

I just remember going into my room, falling to my knees, crying and praying, crying and praying. I didn't know what else to do. Even as I'm writing this, tears are falling from my eyes, just recalling the pain. It's still like a physical pain in my chest just to remember this in my head. Glad to say that all those tears and prayers did not fall on deaf ears.

That's not to say that things were easy 'cause they definitely weren't. Little by little, we made it through, one day at a time. Two years later, we are still living with the effects that all of this trauma and devastation have left us. But here we are, and we have not given up. And now I'm going to tell you how my business helped me heal through this journey.

We have now made it to 2023. It's January, about to be the anniversary of the beginning of a traumatic year. As the mother, grandmother, and leader of my family, I kept thinking to myself, "What do we need?" My heart and mind knew we needed prayer more than anything else. I encouraged my family to pour their hearts out in prayer.

For several months, I only wanted to see my family happy again. Each day, I went to work and showed up for my clients the way I had for over 20 years. Some days, with tears in my eyes; some days, my clients had me laughing to tears. The salon was a place of comfort where I could forget about the pain I was enduring at home. Some clients I had known for years I could share my journey with, and what I received back was love, encouragement, and prayers.

You see, usually, the stylist is the one listening and encouraging. This time, it was me on the receiving end. Then I started to realize that a stylist/client relationship can be an interchange of encouragement. That's exactly what I received, and it was part of my healing journey.

As this journey continued, I was still looking for something to make my family happy again. Being in the beauty industry for over 20 years, I have collected a lot of knowledge on haircare and products that aid in hair health. I've always thought of creating my product line. For some reason, I felt that this was the time. I started to bounce the idea around to my children, close friends, and family. They lit up with excitement! Everyone thought it was a great idea. That gave me the motivation I needed to get started.

So, in January 2023, the product line planning began.

The first thing I did was to secure a coach. I joined her program, *How To Launch Your Product Line in 90 Days*. Although it actually took about six months. One of the biggest things I had to think about was what would this product line be named? I didn't want anything generic. I wanted it to be meaningful.

After a lot of thought about everything that our family had gone through, I wanted to use the name to connect with my granddaughter, who was lost. Her name was Treasure. So, for a few weeks, I played with all the names of "Treasure," looking to see what was taken and what was available, and then I finally came up with the name Tre-Azure. I was so proud; it was so perfect. It was exquisite and precious, just like Treasure.

From that point on, I really gave my all, which I continue to do to this day for this namesake. I will always do my best to have the best products attached to Tre-Azure. On July 4th, 2023, Tre-Azure was officially launched to the public. The line started with three products. We are now at six products. The line has received local awards, such as the 2024 Innovator Award issued by the Madison Black Business Chamber of Commerce.

The salon was a safe space for me between my clients and coworkers. I am now turning some of that pain and tragedy into triumph: something beautiful, wonderful, and a forever namesake. The product line helped my heart heal in places that I don't know exactly how I could've healed otherwise. I'm not sure if it was just a good distraction, but whatever it was, it helped me a lot, and it helped my family.

Though the pain never truly leaves, we've found ways to honor the memory of our loss. Tre-Azure is more than a product line—it's a symbol of resilience, love, and the strength that can emerge from grief. Each day is still a challenge, but we face it with hope, knowing that even in the darkest times, there can be light.

I believe as well. I thank Jehovah for giving me that vision and that help when I needed it.

To conclude, I'd like to offer a piece of advice – **never underestimate the power of faith, family, and perseverance.** Life can throw unimaginable hardships your way, but you are stronger than you think. When things feel overwhelming, remember to take things one day at a time. Lean on your loved ones, trust in God, your inner strength, and know that it's okay to ask for help when you need it.

As you continue to read the stories of resilience in this anthology, here are a few tips to keep in mind:

1. **Pause and Reflect:** Take time to absorb each story. Reflect on how these experiences of loss, growth, and triumph may resonate with your own life.
2. **Find Inspiration:** Every story is proof of our human strength. Use these stories as motivation to push through your own challenges, no matter how big or small.
3. **Embrace Vulnerability:** These authors have shared their most vulnerable moments. Let their courage inspire you to confront your own vulnerabilities and turn them into sources of strength.

4. **Celebrate Resilience:** Life will test you, but resilience is the key to overcoming adversity. Celebrate your victories, no matter how small, and honor the journey of healing and growth.
5. **Pay it Forward:** As these stories inspire and uplift you, consider how you can share your own story or be a source of support for others on their journey.

By carrying these lessons with you, may you find strength in your own path and help others find theirs. Keep moving forward—there's light ahead, even in the darkest moments.

Nina Moorer

CEO Moorer Group

www.ninamoorer.com
www.moorerfit.com
https://www.facebook.com/nina.moorer/
https://www.instagram.com/therealninamoorer/

Nina Moorer, a global entrepreneur, transformational speaker, and lifestyle empowerment coach, rose from humble beginnings in North Philadelphia to become a highly sought-after leader. With candor, tenacity, and grace, Nina transforms lives through her passion for service. From caring for stray animals to navigating motherhood at 15, she has always been driven to make a difference.

In 2014, Nina shifted from a 20-year cosmetology career to become a network marketing and e-commerce expert. She grew a customer base of over 500,000 and earned over two million dollars in sales, gaining recognition in business publications like Business for Home.

As the CEO of Nina Moorer INC, she provides women with tools for personal and professional growth. Nina, passionate about health and wellness after her own battle with obesity, is dedicated to helping others take control of their lives. She and her husband, Paul, are proud parents and grandparents.

My Life Beyond The Chair

By: Nina Moorer

The city of Philadelphia, with its mosaic of neighborhoods and bustling streets, provided the backdrop for my early years and set the stage for my extraordinary journey. Growing up in a community where resilience was not just a trait but a necessity, I faced the unanticipated reality of becoming a teenage mother at 15. This pivotal moment transformed my life from the carefree days of adolescence to the complex challenges of adulthood. With my son's well-being and future in my hands, I knew that the path I chose would shape my destiny and his.

In those formative years, the neighborhood mall became my refuge and a source of inspiration. I would often find myself mesmerized by the nail artists at their booths, creating elaborate designs that turned ordinary nails into art pieces. The intricate patterns and vibrant colors seemed to reflect a world of possibilities. I watched with rapt attention, absorbing every technique and nuance, understanding that this could be my ticket to financial independence.

Despite their unwavering support, my parents provided only the basics—ensuring we had a roof over our heads and meeting our immediate needs. Everything beyond that was up to me. I needed a career that I could start immediately, one that would support my son and allow me to thrive despite the challenges. It became clear that I had a natural gift for working with my hands—a talent that would become the cornerstone of my professional life.

The Bible's promise that "God gave us the ability to create wealth and put it in our hands" resonated deeply with me. I took this to heart, believing that my ability to transform lives through beauty was more than just a skill—it was a divine purpose. embarked on a journey leading me through the vibrant world of cosmetology and beyond.

After graduating from the Philadelphia High School for Girls, I eagerly transitioned into a beauty culture school. The transition from high school to beauty school was swift and seamless. I enrolled at Berean Institute in North Philadelphia, driven by a sense of urgency and determination. I immersed myself in the curriculum, mastering the basics of cosmetology, but I quickly realized that excelling in this field required more than just foundational knowledge. It was about developing a unique style and becoming an expert in my craft.

As I navigated the early stages of my career, I realized that the salon had become my second home. It was a place where I could express my creativity and connect with people profoundly. My reputation grew, and I became known as one city's fastest-growing and most skilled stylists . My clientele began to overflow, providing a stable income and allowing me to support my family and build a life for myself. My work was not just a means to an end; it was a passion that brought joy to me and my clients. The transformation I witnessed in their lives was incredibly rewarding, and I took immense pride in my ability to make them feel beautiful and confident.

At 20, I had my second son, and my life became even more intertwined with my profession. By 26, I was married to a military man, and we relocated away from Philadelphia. Leaving behind my loyal clients was one of the hardest decisions I had ever made. The salon was not just a place of work; it was a sanctuary where I had forged deep relationships and built a community.

The move to a new city and the subsequent adjustments were challenging. I connected with a new church community and other military wives, finding ways to continue honing my skills despite the changes. The feeling of loss was profound; it was as though I was grieving the end of an era. I missed the vibrant energy of Philadelphia and the familiar faces that had become like family. My new circumstances felt like a far cry from what I had left behind.

In San Diego, I briefly experimented with a traditional job, hoping for a change of pace. However, my stint lasted only a week. The paycheck was insufficient to replace the fulfillment I found in the salon. I missed the creative process, the personal connections, and the satisfaction of transforming lives through beauty. It was clear that my heart was still deeply invested in my craft.

Life took another dramatic turn when my eldest daughter was born prematurely, weighing just 1lb 12oz. Her fragile condition and the emotional strain of living far from home made me reassess my priorities. Every day was a struggle as we faced the uncertainty of her health. Once she was stable, I knew it was time to return to Philadelphia. My marriage was also experiencing difficulties, and returning home seemed like the right decision. The prospect of reopening my salon was both exciting and daunting.

A year after moving back, I opened my first salon, "Twice As Nice." This was a new chapter in my life, marked by both excitement and fear. I had never owned a salon before, and opening it shortly before 9/11 brought challenges. The events of September 11th had a profound impact on all of us, and the uncertainty surrounding those times made running a new business even more challenging.

As fate would have it, my ex-husband was called back to active duty, putting additional strain on our marriage. Managing a new salon and going through a divorce was overwhelming. I was engulfed in a whirlwind of emotions and responsibilities, and healing from this tumultuous period felt like an insurmountable task. The pain was intense, but I had no choice but to move forward. The demands of life required resilience, and I drew on every ounce of strength I had.

After closing my salon, I shifted my focus to managing salons around Philadelphia. This role allowed me to stay connected to the industry I loved while navigating new challenges. Managing multiple salons gave me valuable insights into the beauty business's inner workings and honed my leadership skills. I learned that the relationship between a client and their stylist was much deeper than anyone outside the industry might understand.

Clients trust their stylists with more than just their hair; they share their lives, their struggles, and their triumphs. As a stylist, you become a confidant, therapist, and friend. Your clients' stories often reveal more about them than words ever could. Their hair becomes a canvas for their emotions and experiences, a reflection of their inner selves.

My children, whom I affectionately call "salon kids," grew up spending many hours in the salon with me. They did their homework at the shop and often shared meals with me there. My long hours were necessary to build a successful career, but they came with sacrifices. Despite the demanding schedule, I valued the flexibility that allowed me to be a "present mom" for my children. This was a significant benefit of being a cosmetologist, even though it came with its own set of challenges.

The beauty industry was immensely rewarding, but the long hours took their toll on me physically and emotionally. My work ethic and talent were undeniable, but I struggled with personal issues, including poor eating habits and neglecting my own well-being. I didn't realize the extent of these issues until I found myself at a crossroads.

In 2012, I remarried, and in 2014, I gave birth to our youngest daughter. During this pregnancy, I came to a crucial realization: my time behind the salon chair was coming to an end. The long hours required to excel in my profession were no longer sustainable, especially with a growing family to care for.

It was during this period of reflection that network marketing came into my life. One night, while scrolling online, I discovered a detox tea that piqued my interest. What started as a casual exploration soon became a transformative journey. Along with a low-carb lifestyle, I incorporated the supplements from my company and released over 125 lbs. The change in my health was remarkable, and I've successfully kept the weight off. Network marketing didn't just change my life; it saved it. The long hours and physical demands of working in the beauty industry have led to poor health and emotional distress. Network marketing offered a path to financial freedom and personal well-being that I hadn't thought possible.

Network marketing was a revelation. It offered me the flexibility to design my own schedule, which meant I could finally achieve the work-life balance I had always sought. It allowed me to pursue my passions without being tethered to a salon chair. This newfound freedom was invigorating, and I quickly embraced the opportunities that came with it.

With network marketing, I found a new sense of purpose and fulfillment. It allowed me to travel to incredible destinations—Australia, Peru, Jamaica, the Bahamas, Canada, the UK, Trinidad, and more. Each trip was not just a chance to explore new places but also an opportunity to connect with people from diverse backgrounds and share my journey with them. I no longer had to live paycheck to paycheck or miss important family events due to work commitments. The freedom to build a successful business without being tied to a salon chair was liberating.

In January 2015, I retired from the salon industry. This decision was both exhilarating and emotional. It marked the end of one chapter and the beginning of another. By October 2022, I had also retired my husband, a deeply fulfilling milestone. Network marketing has afforded us the financial freedom to live comfortably and make a significant impact on the lives of thousands of people around the world. We achieved multiple millions in earnings and were able to help others find their paths to success and fulfillment through personal development and growth.

One of the most rewarding aspects of network marketing has been the ability to coach others toward true transformation in their weight loss journeys. I have seen firsthand how people's lives can change when they adopt healthier habits and embrace a new mindset. The success stories are a testament to the power of resilience and the potential for positive change.

Looking back, I have no regrets about my days behind the chair. My career as a cosmetologist profoundly shaped me , teaching me resilience, creativity, and the importance of human connection. The salon was where I learned to balance artistry with empathy, where I discovered that the true value of my work lay in the joy and confidence I brought to others.

But finding true freedom and purpose beyond the salon chair has been one of the most rewarding experiences of my life. Network marketing gave me the opportunity to create a life of meaning and impact, allowing me to build a legacy for my family and help others along the way. The journey has been filled with challenges and triumphs, each step contributing to a larger narrative of growth and transformation.

If my story serves any purpose, I hope it inspires others to pursue their own paths and discover their true purpose. There is indeed life beyond the chair—one that is filled with opportunities, freedom, and the chance to make a difference in the world. Embrace your journey, follow your passions, and never underestimate the power of your gifts. Your story is uniquely yours, and it has the potential to inspire others to find their own path to fulfillment and success.

The lessons I have learned along the way—resilience in the face of adversity, the value of hard work, and the importance of staying true to oneself—are not just personal experiences but universal truths. They are the principles that have guided me through each phase of my life, from the early days of struggling as a teenage mother to the triumphs of building a successful network marketing business.

In sharing my journey, I hope to encourage others to find their calling, seek growth opportunities, and embrace the challenges that come their way. Life is a series of chapters, each one building on the last. Embrace each chapter with an open heart and a willingness to learn, and you will find that your story, too, can be one of incredible transformation and success.

My journey is a testament to the power of perseverance, the importance of following one's passion, and the profound impact of discovering one's true purpose. I encourage you to take your own leap of faith, explore new horizons, and create a fulfilling and meaningful life.. Your story, like mine, has the potential to inspire and transform not just your own life but the lives of those around you.

Kiara Allen

CEO - K'Cheveux

https://www.facebook.com/kiara.allen1

Owner and CEO of K'CHEVEUX, a renowned salon in Madison, Wisconsin, where she provides a wide range of services, including custom color for wigs and hair extensions, haircuts, lightening, toning, protective styles, natural hair care, and more. With over 12 years of experience in the hair industry, Kiara specializes in all hair types and addresses challenges such as hair loss, thinning, and balding. Born and raised in Chicago, Illinois, Kiara is also a mother of three, an entrepreneur, and a wife.

Her passion for hair lies in helping clients look and feel their best, and her goal is to bring every client's vision to life, boosting their confidence with healthy, beautiful hair. Beyond her work in the salon, Kiara is dedicated to giving back to the community, particularly supporting the youth with love, guidance, and hope. She also helped break barriers by contributing to the passing of the Hair Braiding Bill in Madison, allowing unlicensed stylists to earn an income from braiding and natural styles, celebrating the cultural significance of these practices.

Phenomenally Blessed

By: Kiara Allen

My name is Kiara Allen. I was born and raised in Chicago, Illinois. My mother was a single mother of five girls, me being the oldest. Sometimes, she did have the help of my only known biological uncle, Derrick, when needed. We went through a lot of challenges in Chicago, such as poverty and homelessness.

In 2002, my uncle Derrick moved us from Chicago to Madison, Wisconsin. It was a lovely, peaceful, diverse, and family-friendly breath of fresh air. My mother was a great mother who always did her best to raise five girls independently.

My favorite memory with my mom was our bonding time when she would do our hair. My mother took pride in growing, maintaining, and styling our hair. She never went to school for hair, but braiding was her natural talent. My mother was so good at braiding hair that other parents began asking her to do their children's hair around the neighborhood.

If you must know, having a bomb hairdo and healthy hair is central to our culture. So, I fell in love with getting my hair done and always wanted the best of any trending hairstyle. It then became a side income for my mom. She had started charging for her braiding services, and people would pay. To top it off, she was also great at growing hair.

She had difficulty getting a great job with no GED or high school diploma. She had dropped out of school because she became pregnant with me at the age of 16. So it was dope and helpful that she could make money from her natural talent. This became a nice source of income.

As a child, I was a natural-born entrepreneur. My dream was to become the world's greatest fashion designer. I loved making others look good because if you look good, you feel good. The beauty industry was just everything to me and a dope way to express yourself through fashion. After watching my mother make money from doing hair, it clicked in my mind that I could learn and begin making money from doing hair.

I had always had an urge that it was meant for me to be my own boss and be wealthy with multiple successful businesses. It all started when I was eleven years old. I would make flyers in the teacher's lounge at school or the library, go around nice-looking neighborhoods, and pass them out. I would rake leaves and care for plants, mow the lawns, shovel snow, clean garages, and remove crab apples from yards for money. It made me lots of money, but it only lasted for so long before the world became increasingly unsafe for a child to walk around door to door alone. So, my mother became stricter and stopped me from doing these services immediately.

At sixteen, I obtained my third real-life job and disliked it so much. I then realized I was helping this company make millions and making their dreams come true while they were paying me pennies. I became fed up with working for others.

My hunger for entrepreneurship grew stronger and stronger, so I began researching everything about business and the beauty industry. I was a teen with huge dreams and even bigger goals. It wasn't long before my aunt Coreatta gave me my first colorful weave, which my mom was against because of my age. The colors were bold and loud, which my mom felt was distasteful and inappropriate for my age. My mom always encouraged us that natural beauty is everything. I agree, but that first weave had fireworks going off in my mind. I fell in love and wanted to learn more.

Eventually, my aunt taught me to do what they call 27-piece pixie cuts and styles, quick weaves, sew-ins, and crochet. Her best friend, Shunte, also like an aunt, taught me to braid and perfect my craft.

They both always said they saw something great in me. Shunte stayed challenging me. I remember one time she was over at my aunt Coreatta's house doing her hair, and they called me into the room, looked at me with a sly grin, and said, "It's time to put you to the test. You have all these sewing certificates; you should know how to do a sew-in." I was stunned and intrigued at the same time. I took the challenge and smoked it. They were impressed, and in a few months, they told their friends about me and other family members. My clientele began picking up.

For my family members and friends, I wouldn't charge them because I used them to practice new trends, techniques, and styles. The more you practice, the better you become. There's a saying in the hair industry: you haven't mastered something unless you've done it one hundred times or more.

I eventually went to hair school in 2018 and graduated in 2019. I am now a mother of three amazing children, married to my partner of ten years, and a licensed cosmetologist. I have now been in the hair industry for twelve years and counting. I still take classes and educate myself because, as we all know, it's a fast-growing and changing industry. There's always a new trend every time you look up. Right now, hairstylists are in high demand.

In my community in Madison, there's a huge lack of black culture, meaning Madison doesn't have the cultural expressions of black people. Black culture affects society greatly, encouraging better citizenship, unity, community building, understanding, and identity formation. There are not a lot of resources here for black people, such as resources to help us thrive, and there is no black history, art, museums, fashion, music, etc. Madison isn't a huge city like Atlanta or Chicago, where black culture thrives. So there were only a few stylists when I started out, but now there are so many, and still some emerging, which I think is dope. The universe has plenty of abundance and prosperity for everyone. We have some dope stylists here in Madison; there's no competition between most of us, and most of us support each other, which I love because unity is key. I do believe we badly need more black culture and fashion here in Madison.

The lack of black culture and fashion limits the community's opportunities to thrive and excel in Madison. When I say that, it limits equality, makes it hard to escape poverty and build wealth here in Madison, and limits the youth's sense of self-love and identity. Black culture emphasizes community, solidarity, and social justice. Living in a place with a thriving black culture would mean no barriers or limits to anything. It would create more jobs, careers, leaders, unity, and generational wealth.

Being a licensed cosmetologist, I can always have a great source of income, and there are so many career paths and opportunities I have had and still have to come within this industry. It's fascinating and a blessing. To this day, this is my main source of income, and I am a part-time instructor at the first black-owned hair school here in Madison, "Chanell Ardor." This industry has so many options; you will never be without income.

I always say follow your heart, make goals for yourself regularly, unity is key, be phenomenal in everything you do, do your best, keep educating yourself, and be passionate about everything you do.

I became aware of who I was at an early age because my Uncle Derrick taught me my roots, spirituality, and the universe and how unique and attuned we humans are with the universe and nature. I became very intrigued at 11 and began studying entrepreneurship, leadership, wealth, the universe, astrology, and much more. It sparked something in me that made me want more out of life, especially coming from poverty in Chicago. I felt I had to be the one to change my family's situation. I always knew I wanted to be a boss of some sort, running my own business.

With those desires came challenges, self-discipline, leadership, knowing myself, business knowledge, etc. Most importantly, you must be okay with failing and cannot give up. You can start over as many times as you want until you get it right. You must be willing to take risks and fully invest in yourself mentally, physically, and financially.

I did just that. I started my first business at 11 years old with flyers, which was a success. But I started thinking about my future and what I wanted to be growing up. I knew it wasn't an employee at all. I knew I wanted to be the boss and be in the beauty industry. Beauty has no limits; it never goes away. It's always in high demand because who doesn't want to look or feel beautiful?

My advice is to find what you love to do and be good at it or invest in yourself to perfect it. You have to educate yourself on business, write goals, sit and learn, and think deeply about what impact you want to leave on this planet. Who do I want to be? You have to own it, know it before seeing it with your own eyes, believe in yourself even if no one else does, and go for it. You cannot let fear hold you back at all. You cannot be afraid to fail because it will happen, and when it does, think about the bigger picture, don't rush, pick yourself up, and go for it again and again until you get it right where you desire.

Self-love and care help build that confidence, too. When I say self-love and care, I mean to love you for you no matter who doesn't, be unapologetic about being your authentic self, groom yourself regularly, show up and out for yourself, don't doubt yourself, and be grateful too, because things can always be worse. Everyone is here for a reason: to thrive and elevate.

Choya Woods

Founder Melanin Beauty Bar

Melanin.glossgenius.com
https://www.facebook.com/choya.woods
Instagram.com/melanin.beautybar

Choya Woods, a Chicago native and Scientific College of Beauty and Barbering graduate, is a seasoned salon owner, hair extension specialist, and devoted wife and mother of four sons. With over a decade of experience, including at a prominent LaCrosse salon, Choya founded Melanin Beauty Bar to create a deliberately inclusive space celebrating diversity. Inspired by the belief that "Melanin" represents the essence of beauty, her salon embraces the natural and varied beauty in everyone.

Melanin Beauty Bar emphasizes cultural motivation and uniqueness, partnering with top stylists and educators from major cities and using high-quality products from international and local vendors to serve its diverse clientele.

The Goddess and the Dragon: Unleashing My Sacred Power

By: Choya Woods

Humboldt Park, a vibrant and resilient neighborhood in Chicago, was where I learned the meaning of responsibility as the eldest of eleven siblings and cousins. I grew up in Humboldt Park, a vibrant neighborhood in Chicago, Illinois. As the eldest of eleven siblings and cousins, I carried significant responsibility from a young age. Raised by my mother and my superhero, Great Grandmother Esther Lites, I was deeply influenced by the strong women in my life. Esther, who was Shoshone Indian and Black, had the most beautiful hair and symbolized resilience and grace

Journal Prompt: Think about the people who have shaped your life the most—whether family members, friends, mentors, or even public figures. What qualities do they possess that you admire?

How have they influenced your view of strength, resilience, or compassion?

How have their actions and words guided your decisions, especially in tough moments?

Are there any specific lessons or mantras they've passed down to you that you carry with you? How have these lessons impacted your personal growth?

But my childhood was marred by sexual abuse, which left me struggling with self-worth and respect for men. This trauma led to a period of promiscuity and a profound sense of bitterness. However, my life took a pivotal turn when I met Demetrius, my husband, and became a mother earlier than expected. The birth of my four sons—Jalen, Jhakai, Jayuant, and Jhamari—catalyzed my transformation. I knew I had to rise above my past to create a legacy of strength and love for my "five kings."

Journal Prompt: Reflect on a moment or series of events that changed the course of your life. What decisions did you make that led to growth or transformation?

Did this event challenge or reinforce your beliefs and values? How?

What internal or external obstacles did you face during this turning point? How did you overcome them?

How do you envision the legacy you are building for future generations or those around you? What steps are you taking today to ensure this legacy lives on?

Despite my challenging beginnings, I was determined to be better for my family. I refused to let the bitterness from my past stain my sons' future. Instead, I channeled my energy into breaking the cycle of pain and building a life filled with purpose and positivity.

As I navigated the complexities of motherhood and personal growth, I found solace and strength in my passion for beauty and self-care. This passion led to the birth of Melanin Beauty Bar, a sanctuary where women could feel empowered and appreciated. The journey of establishing Melanin Beauty Bar was filled with initial struggles and significant milestones. Each challenge I faced only fueled my resolve to create a space where everyone, especially women of African descent, could shine brightly without fear of judgment.

Journal Prompt: What passions or dreams are you pursuing? What challenges have you faced in bringing them to life, and how have you overcome them?

What dreams or passions excite you the most? How do they align with your values, and what role do they play in shaping your future?

Think of when you've felt most alive and connected to your purpose. What dream were you chasing in those moments

How clearly do you see the path toward your dreams? Write down what success looks like for you in pursuing your passion. How do you imagine your life, your work, or your relationships changing once you achieve it?

What obstacles have stood in your way, either from within (fear, doubt, lack of motivation) or external factors (financial constraints, lack of time, resources, or support)? Be honest with yourself about the biggest roadblocks you've encountered.

My ability to "handle things" had become one of my defining qualities. No matter how turbulent life's storms got, I always found a way to navigate through them. But one fateful day at work, my resilience was put to the test.

I was busy with my clients when a woman I had never met before entered the room. There was something almost otherworldly about her presence. She had the strength of ten gods, and her entrance was so quiet that it was as if she had materialized out of thin air. Her mere presence turned my face red without a touch, leaving me breathless and disoriented.

This mysterious figure was Ayohc, a personification of my anxiety. Ayohc had always been there, lurking in the shadows, manifesting as a tightening chest, shallow breaths, and an overwhelming dread. It was a magic I didn't know I needed—a gift I never understood.

Journal Prompt: When anxiety shows up in your life, what are the most noticeable signs or triggers? Do certain situations, people, or places increase your anxiety?

How does anxiety impact your thoughts and decisions? Does it influence how you interact with others or how you see yourself?

If you were to give your anxiety a name or a personality, what would it look and feel like? Imagine its colors, shape, voice, or even the space it occupies within you.

What message does your anxiety have for you, and how could this message guide you in your growth?

Mental health is often a difficult topic of conversation in the BIPOC community. We tend to "deal with it" in silence, carrying the weight of our struggles alone. For years, I did the same. I kept Ayohc hidden, ashamed of the panic attacks, the dread that would creep up on me unbidden. But naming my anxiety was the most freeing thing I ever did. It allowed me to take something that's a part of me and see it outside of myself, like Picture in Picture—something surreal yet empowering.

Journal Prompt: Reflect on your mental health journey. Have you ever named your emotions or struggles? How did that change your relationship with them?

Think about the emotions that have been most difficult for you to confront. Have you ever given them a name, face, or identity?

How did naming or identifying these emotions make them feel more manageable? Did it allow you to approach them differently?

How have your strategies for managing difficult emotions changed over time? Do you have specific tools or practices (e.g., meditation, writing, talking to others) that have helped you?

What emotions or mental health challenges do you still struggle to name, and how might naming them offer you more control or insight?

For years, Ayohc's sudden appearances had thrown me into panic. I struggled to maintain my composure, often retreating to the break room to calm myself. These anxiety attacks were like battles with an invisible force, a goddess who seemed to appear whenever I was playing small. But that day was different. In the midst of my overwhelming anxiety, I looked into the bathroom mirror, my face wet and my shirt drenched from splashing water in a desperate attempt to regain control. I met Ayohc's eyes in the reflection and, for the first time, saw not just a source of fear but a call to greatness.

Journal Prompt: Think about a moment when you faced a difficult emotion head-on. What did you see or understand about yourself in that moment? How did it change you? Recall a time when you experienced a particularly intense or challenging emotion. What caused it, and how did you initially react?

When you faced the emotion head-on, what realizations or insights surfaced? Did you discover new strengths, vulnerabilities, or coping mechanisms within yourself?

What did this experience teach you about your ability to handle adversity? Did it shift how you perceive your resilience or capacity for growth?

How do you handle difficult emotions now compared to how you handled them in the past? What role do these experiences play in your overall personal growth?

"Goddess," Ayohc whispered, her voice deep and resonant, like a distant echo through a canyon. It carried weight and authority, yet there was a softness to it—a gentle hum that seemed to vibrate through the air. Her opalescent aura began to shimmer around her as she spoke, casting a soft, ethereal glow that bathed the room in a calming light. It was as if the very air around me was infused with her presence, soothing the chaos in my mind and heart. I realized that Ayohc was not just my anxiety but also a part of myself that demanded acknowledgment and respect.

Journal Prompt: How have you transformed over time? What aspects of yourself have you come to embrace as powerful and necessary, even if they were once sources of fear or doubt?

Reflect on a time when you were afraid of stepping into your full potential. What were the fears holding you back? How did you confront or overcome them, and how has facing those fears allowed you to grow? How has your understanding of fear evolved over time?

Often, what we view as weaknesses are actually our greatest sources of strength. Consider moments when vulnerability, openness, or softness became powerful tools for connection or healing. How has embracing these qualities changed the way you see yourself and your relationships?

Are there parts of yourself that you once hid from others, fearing judgment or rejection? How have you learned to embrace and celebrate your authentic self, regardless of what others might think? What internal shifts allowed you to reclaim these parts of yourself as powerful and necessary?

My path was never straight; there were mountains, hills, oceans, and trenches. But the light that is mine was always there to guide me. Elevation creates evolution, and we must do both. Just as a dragon might have once been a lion and a lion once an eagle, we must MOVE. Change growth—they are mandatory. Yes, the caves we throw ourselves into are comfortable and safe, and we can thrive in the dark. But there's life in the light.

Journal Prompt: What "caves" do you find yourself retreating into? What would stepping out into the light and embracing change and growth take? Consider the habits, thoughts, or situations you retreat into when life feels overwhelming.

Are these caves of comfort productive, or do they keep you stuck?

What fears or uncertainties keep you from stepping out of these caves? Are they related to past experiences, fear of failure, or something else?

What does "stepping into the light" look like for you? What specific steps or mindset shifts would help you embrace growth and change, even if it feels uncomfortable?

Imagine what your life would look like if you fully embraced change. What would you achieve, and how would it transform your relationships, work, and sense of self?

Ayohc often pushed me to MOVE. Her aura would intensify, colors swirling and shifting like a living thing, encouraging me to take action to step into my power. She had become the superpower of all superpowers. She is mystical! The dragon of all dragons. Crystalline with an opalescent aura. Gentle yet beastly, bold but subtle. Her scales shimmered like labradorite, and her claws were sharpened obsidian. Approachable yet untouchable. She embodied all the best parts of me.

Journal Prompt: Who or what pushes you to move forward? How does this force help you step into your power? What does your "dragon" look like?

Identify the people, experiences, or inner drives that compel you to move forward when you feel stagnant or unsure. What or who lights a fire within you?

How do these influences help you rediscover or step into your own power? In what ways do they push you to grow beyond your current limitations?

Imagine your personal "dragon"—the representation of your inner strength, courage, and resilience. How would it look, move, and act in your life? How do you embody this dragon when challenges arise?

What would it take for you to fully embrace and unleash the power of your "dragon" in every area of your life?

"I see you," I said to my reflection, my voice steady and resolute. "Not only do I see you, but I feel you, and I understand." As I've grown with Ayohc, I've come to know that the Dragon is me—I'm that crystalline dragon with the opalescent aura and the labradorite scales. I'm elegantly fierce; the fire I breathe is the passion and love that burns inside me.

Needing to clear my head, I escaped the grind and got some fresh air. I packed my belongings and took a drive to a secluded forest retreat I had heard about. I hoped to find clarity and peace away from the city's hustle.

The forest was a sanctuary. Tall trees stretched toward the sky, their leaves rustling softly in the wind. The air was fresh and filled with the earthy scent of moss and pine. As I walked along a winding path,

I felt Ayohc's presence, but it was different here—less heavy, more like a quiet companion.

At the retreat, I immersed myself in the natural world, reconnecting with the earth in ways I had never done before. I listened to the powerful rhythms of African chants, letting their deep, ancestral vibrations resonate through my body. When the rain came, I danced in it, feeling the cool droplets cleanse me of lingering doubts and fears.

Journal Prompt: How does nature affect your mental and emotional state? Reflect on a time when connecting with nature brought you peace or clarity.

Consider times when you've felt overwhelmed, anxious, or stressed and how spending time in nature helped you reset. Whether it was a walk in the park, sitting by the ocean, or simply observing the trees outside your window, how did nature provide relief or a new perspective? What is it about nature that allows you to let go of stress and be present in the moment?

Reflect on a moment when connecting with nature gave you clarity. Perhaps you were facing a difficult decision, navigating a personal challenge, or feeling uncertain about your path. How did being in nature—whether through its stillness or its vastness—help you gain perspective or insight into what you needed to do next?

Many people feel a deep, energetic connection to the earth. How do you feel when you touch the ground, lie in the grass, or swim in a natural body of water? Do you sense a grounding energy that helps stabilize your thoughts and emotions? How can you connect with this energy more often in your daily life to bring more calm and balance?

How can you bring the peace and clarity that nature provides into your everyday life, even if you don't always have access to outdoor spaces? What small practices—such as tending to a plant, opening a window to let in fresh air, or taking short mindful walks—can help you maintain that connection to nature and its calming influence?

I dug holes in the soft earth, grounding myself by burying my feet in the mud, feeling the earth's energy rise up through me. The vibrations of singing bowls played in the background, their tones mingling with the rustling leaves and flowing water, creating a symphony of nature and sound that soothed my soul.

Journal Prompt: What practices help you feel grounded and connected to the earth? How do these practices help you manage stress or anxiety?

In moments of solitude, I bathed in sunlight, naked, letting the warmth embrace me and heal the wounds that had festered in the shadows for so long. The sun's rays felt like a blessing, a reminder that I was alive, vibrant, and connected to something much greater than myself.

Journal Prompt: Reflect on the moments when you felt most connected to yourself and the world around you. What were the circumstances, and how did they change you?

One evening, I felt the pull to visit a nearby river. The transition from the quiet forest to the rushing waters was jarring yet soothing. I walked along the riverbank, the water lapping at my feet, the cool breeze filling my lungs. Ayohc's presence was there too, a gentle hum in the background of my thoughts, her voice now a soothing melody, blending with the sounds of nature. Once vibrant and powerful, her aura softened into a subtle glow that seemed to merge with the twilight as if she were a part of the world around me.

Journal Prompt: Consider a time when you felt in tune with the natural world. What emotions or thoughts surfaced? How did this connection influence your perspective on life?

I found a secluded spot and sat down, watching the river flow under the moonlight. I pulled out a small crystal from my bag, a gift from a local crystal shop I frequented. It was a piece of amethyst known for its calming properties. Holding it in my hand, I felt a surge of energy, a connection to something greater than myself.

"Thanks for having my back," I whispered to Ayohc. Her voice responded, soft yet firm, "You're learning to trust yourself." It was like the gentle rustling of leaves, calming yet profound. "And in doing so, you're finding the balance between fear and courage, between pain and joy." As she spoke, her aura expanded, embracing me in warmth and light, leaving me feeling safe and protected.

Journal Prompt: Reflect on a time when you felt supported by something greater than yourself—whether it was a person, a belief, or a force of nature. How did this support help you move forward?

I smiled, feeling a deep sense of peace. I realized that my journey with Ayohc was not about overcoming anxiety but about embracing it as a part of my path. The city, the river, the chants, the sunlight—all these elements were helping me understand this truth.

Journal Prompt: What elements in your life help you understand and embrace your challenges? How do they contribute to your personal growth?

My journey toward self-love and healing was not one I walked alone. At the heart of it all were the people I loved the most—my husband, Demetrius, and our four sons, Jalen, Jhakai, Jayuant, and Jhamari. They were my anchors, the ones who gave me strength when I felt like I had none.

Journal Prompt: Reflect on the role your loved ones play in your life. How do they support you, and how do you support them in return?

When I first met Demetrius, I was a young woman still grappling with the shadows of my past. I had been hurt, and that pain had shaped how I viewed myself and others. Trust didn't come easily to me, especially not with men. But Demetrius was different. He had a patience and gentleness that disarmed me. Where I expected judgment or distance, he offered understanding and warmth.

Journal Prompt: Think about someone who has helped you heal. What qualities did they bring into your life that made a difference?

Our relationship wasn't perfect; we had our struggles. There were moments when my old wounds would surface, threatening to undermine the love we were building. But Demetrius never wavered. He saw the parts of me that I tried to hide—the fear, the insecurities, the anxiety—and loved me anyway. He was my mirror in many ways, reflecting back to me the person I could become if only I embraced my inner strength.

Together, we learned the importance of communication, of being open about our feelings and fears. Demetrius taught me that vulnerability wasn't a weakness but a bridge to a deeper connection. It was through this vulnerability that I began to heal, to see myself as worthy of love—not just from him but from myself.

Journal Prompt: How has vulnerability played a role in your relationships? What have you learned about yourself through being open and honest with those you love?

Becoming a mother changed everything. When Jalen was born, I felt an overwhelming sense of responsibility—not just for his physical well-being but for the emotional and spiritual legacy I was passing on. I knew that the bitterness and pain I carried from my past could not be allowed to taint the future I wanted for my sons.

Journal Prompt: Reflect on a time when a major life change made you reassess your priorities. How did this change influence your growth?

Each of my sons brought something unique into my life. Jalen, the eldest, was my first lesson in patience and unconditional love. Jhakai's curiosity and energy reminded me of the importance of staying present and engaged in the world around me. Jayuant, with his sensitivity, taught me to embrace my emotions rather than suppress them. And Jhamari, the youngest, was my reminder that joy could be found even in the smallest moments.

As they grew, so did I. Motherhood wasn't just about teaching my sons how to navigate the world; it was about learning from them, too. They were my greatest teachers, showing me the importance of resilience, forgiveness, and the power of love to heal even the deepest wounds.

Journal Prompt: What lessons have you learned from the people you care for? How have these lessons shaped who you are today?

One of the greatest challenges I faced as a mother was breaking the cycle of pain that had been passed down through generations. I was determined that my sons would not inherit the bitterness or trauma that had once consumed me. I wanted them to grow up in a home filled with love, respect, and the freedom to express themselves.

This meant confronting my own demons head-on. I had to learn how to forgive—not just those who had hurt me, but also myself. I had to let go of the guilt and shame that had kept me in a cycle of self-doubt. It wasn't easy, but it was necessary. I couldn't teach my sons to love themselves if I couldn't model that love myself.

Journal Prompt: Consider the cycles or patterns you want to break in your life. What steps can you take to create a new legacy for yourself and those you love?

Like any other family, ours faced its share of challenges. There were moments of financial stress, health scares, and the inevitable conflicts that come with raising children. But through it all, we remained united. Demetrius and I made a conscious decision to face every challenge as a team, to communicate openly with our sons about what was happening, and to lean on each other for support.

One of the most important lessons we imparted to our sons was the value of resilience. Life would not always be easy, but they had the strength within them to overcome any obstacle. We encouraged them to see challenges not as setbacks but as opportunities for growth.

Journal Prompt: Think about a time when your family or loved ones faced a challenge together. How did you support each other through it, and what did you learn from the experience?

Amidst the struggles, there were countless moments of joy that made everything worthwhile. Watching Jalen's first performance, seeing

Jhakai's first dunk, feeling pride in Jayuant's success on the track, and holding Jhamari close after a long day were the moments that filled my heart with love and gratitude.

Journal Prompt: What small moments bring you joy in your relationships? How can you be more present to appreciate these moments?

As a mother, these moments reminded me that life is not just about the big milestones; it's about the everyday acts of love and connection. It's about being there for each other through the highs and the lows and celebrating the journey together.

Journal Prompt: Reflect on how you can cultivate more joy and presence in your daily life. What small changes can you make to be more connected to your loved ones?

In the end, my journey of self-love and healing was deeply intertwined with my role as a wife and mother. Through the love and support of Demetrius and our sons, I found the strength to embrace my inner being, to pour into myself, and to become the healed version of me—the god self that could pour light and love into the world.

Journal Prompt: How has your family or support system helped you become the person you are today? Reflect on how you can continue growing and healing within these relationships.

As I continue to grow and inspire others, I carry with me the lessons learned from my family: the importance of resilience, the power of love, and the beauty of embracing every part of who we are. This is the legacy I leave for my sons and the light I share with the world.

Journal Prompt: What legacy are you building through your relationships? How can you nurture this legacy to create a lasting impact?

My ancestors are always with me, guiding me as I navigate my path. They have inspired Melanin Beauty Bar, which has become more than just a beauty business—it's a sanctuary. From the moment someone steps through the door, they are wrapped in warmth, like a comforting embrace from an elder.

At Melanin Beauty Bar, we focus on healing—external beauty or internal transformation. Every service is done with intention, and every product is chosen with care. The scent of the oils and the soothing ambiance we create to honor the wisdom and love passed down through generations.

Journal Prompt: What spaces in your life offer you comfort and healing? How can you bring more of that into your daily routine?

Melanin Beauty Bar is a survivor's survivor. It's my dream realized in today's reality, and it's my grandchildren's head start. No matter what life throws at us, we all have superpowers. These aren't just the powers to endure but also to transform, heal, and create. I've learned that unlocking these powers lies in self-awareness and self-love.

I encourage you to take a moment, write your name backward, and see it as a reflection and a symbol of the goddess within you. Name your anxiety and insecurities and claim them as part of your power. When you shine your light on your darkest parts, you reveal the incredible strength that was always there, waiting to be acknowledged.

Remember, you were hiding in the dark all along—the powerful, beautiful force ready to step into the light. So, shine your light on yourself, embrace every part of who you are, and know you can do anything.

With love,

Choya Rose

Aleisha Kuntu

Coach Boss Beautii Boutique

https://www.instagram.com/boss_beautii_/

Aleisha Kuntu is a dedicated single mother of three boys who mean the world to her. As a community health worker and recovery coach, she is passionate about helping others, a passion rooted in her own journey with substance abuse. With the love and support of her children, Aleisha overcame her addiction and has been sober for six years.

Her personal experiences have profoundly shaped who she is today, and she finds great fulfillment in guiding others toward healthier, more meaningful lives. Aleisha's story is one of resilience, love, and the transformative power of community support.

Lost in the Nightlife: Finding Myself Again

By: Aleisha Kuntu

I never thought I would be so vulnerable with myself that I would be telling my story, not only telling my story but also telling my story to the world. I used to be so embarrassed by my past that I shamed myself for the things I did and the things I went through. If I knew what I knew now, I would be on every stage telling my story to anyone wanting to listen.

I now give myself grace and a lot of self-talk, reminding myself where I have been and where I'm going. I no longer let my past define me, nor do I sit and judge myself about it anymore. Yes, I always judged myself at the beginning of my journey and never had anything positive to say to myself. Sounds crazy, right? Well, that is what it's like when you let others fill your head with negative words about yourself. Yes, you read that right; I let how others thought and what others said about me build me into a negative person. I know you want to know now, like, "Girl, what you been out here doin' in these streets?"

So, like, my whole addiction thing started off pretty chill. YES, I said addiction!! It was just some nights out and parties, you know? Nothing too crazy at first. I would go out only on the weekends, Fridays, and Saturdays for a few drinks and in by midnight, and that's it.

Next thing you know, I'm no longer keeping track of how many drinks I'm having. I'm no longer chasing my drinks with water; I am taking shots with mixed drinks and drinking until bar time. I started hanging out with all types of crowds of people; what can I say? I was what they call a drunk social butterfly; the crowds loved me, and I loved that "me," too. Well, at least I thought that I did.

The whole nightlife scene and this fake sense of being super tight with people, I thought, were where my friends totally took over. I started to find a reason to go out any day of the week. I was out Wing Wednesday, Thirsty Thursday, Fu*k IT Friday, and Shot Night Saturdays. Yes, we had a name for our party days because we loved them, and who doesn't nickname things they love?

I started going to people's houses after bar time to party, letting anybody, including strangers, come to my house after the bars. I eventually was introduced to the party drugs. We called them exotic uppers during my days—Molly, cocaine, and ecstasy.

I would sometimes mix them up, take all three of them on the same night, and be up for days off of my exotic cocktails. In the beginning, I could function off of them and be able to drink all night and still get ready for work, but that didn't last long. I eventually would crash and sleep for two days straight.

I mean, I was staying up all night, doing drugs and drinking, and just ignoring all my responsibilities. Eventually, everything I had worked hard for was gone. My job? Gone. My family? Neglected. My well-being? Yeah, that was out the window. It was like I was sacrificing everything at the altar for my addiction that I didn't even realize I had an addiction until it became too late.

Man, the consequences were hitting me from left to right, and they were hitting me hard. When I lost my job, it felt like the ground had fallen out from under me. The stability I had depended on was gone, and with it went any sense of control over my life. I could feel my relationships slipping away too. Every lie I told to cover up my addiction felt like another brick in the wall I was building between me and my family.

And the worst part was, I didn't know how to stop. The shame was suffocating, and I felt like I was drowning in my own choices. Constantly lying to my family about where I was and what I was doing. I never wandered the streets homeless because I knew I had kids, so part of me was still there; I wasn't totally gone yet.

My kids, who deserved a stable and loving parent, were stuck with this grumpy, unreliable mother. Mornings were the absolute worst. I'd wake up with these killer hangovers and this desperate need for another "exotic cocktail" just to get through the day. It was like being trapped in this never-ending cycle of misery, to be honest.

One day, I just hit this breaking point. I was so tired of all the lies, the deceit, and feeling like I was stuck in this endless loop of addiction. I remember one particular morning when I looked at my kids, and the weight of everything hit me. They were playing, completely unaware of my internal battle, and I realized that they were my reason to fight.

The love I felt for them was overwhelming, and I knew, in that moment, that if I could die for them, I could live for them too. That realization became my anchor on the hardest days. "If I could die for them, why couldn't I live for them?" My mom's words kept echoing in my mind, and I knew it was time to make a change. It wouldn't be easy, but I had to do it for them, myself, and my mother.

I didn't need any interventions, nor did I feel like I needed rehab to get through my turning point. I just knew I needed to do it.

So, I started my journey to recovery by diving into knowledge and inspiration. I spent hours at the library while my children were at school, reading everything I could about addiction and recovery. I changed the music I was listening to, too, and would wake up in the morning listening to inspirational stories from people all over the world who overcame addiction, too.

I found this love in the words of Sarah Jakes Roberts on YouTube. Her podcasts were like a lifeline for me. There was one podcast episode where Sarah Jakes Roberts said, 'Your past is not a prison, it's a lesson.' That line stuck with me. I realized that I had been holding myself prisoner to my mistakes, letting my past control me.

Her words helped me see that my past was not something to be ashamed of, but something to learn from and grow beyond. From that point on, I stopped letting my past define me, and I started to rebuild my life. It was like she was speaking directly to me, telling me that I could do this and turn my life around. I believed her, and I also believed in myself.

Of course, it wasn't all smooth sailing. Initially, I gave up a few times and was like I can manage this; I can go back to only going out on weekends and maybe only if I would just have some drinks and no exotic cocktails. Then, I realized I had no self-control and would start my journey again.

Yes, there were days when I felt like giving up when the social butterfly would want to come out and play with those not-so-good friends, and nights when the craving for those exotic cocktails was so intense that I didn't know if I could keep resisting them. Still, I did; I kept reminding myself of why I was doing this and who I was doing it for.

I thought about my kids and how much they needed me. I thought about the life I wanted to build for us, a life free from the chains of addiction. And that kept me going, even on the hardest days.

I also realized that I couldn't do this alone. I needed a support system, people who understood what I was going through and could offer encouragement and advice. I joined an online support group and found a community of people on the same journey as me. We shared our struggles and victories, which made a huge difference. Knowing that I wasn't alone and that others understood and cared gave me the strength to keep going.

I'll never forget my first support group meeting. I logged in, feeling nervous and unsure, but the minute I started listening to others share their stories, I felt an overwhelming sense of relief. For the first time in what felt like forever, I wasn't alone. Hearing the struggles of others who had been in my shoes made me feel seen and understood.

Their victories became my motivation, and their words of encouragement gave me the strength to keep going.

As I got closer to my first year of sobriety and started to rebuild myself, I decided it was time to invest in myself. I started Boss Beautii Boutique, selling eyelashes from my home. I applied them for my customers, dropped them off, and shipped them out. However, they needed it or wanted it, baby, I was going to do it.

This venture gave me a sense of purpose and pride that I had never felt before. I was building something positive, something I could be proud of other than my amazing children. It was like I was finally taking control of my life and creating a future I could be excited about.

As I continued on my path to recovery, I started to rediscover the joy in life. I found happiness in the little things, like spending time with my kids, working on my business, and being present. I realized that I didn't need drugs or alcohol to feel good. The world had so much beauty and joy, and I could finally see it.

Now, I'm looking forward to the future with hope and excitement. I know there will be challenges, but I also know I have the strength and support to overcome them. I'm building a life that I'm proud of, a life that my kids can be proud of. And that makes all the hard work worth it.

My journey into addiction was a dark and difficult one, but it taught me that my future is brighter than my past was. Throughout this journey, I learned so much about myself and what I'm capable of. It showed me the importance of love, resilience, and the power of change. I'm not the same person I was before, and for that, I'm grateful. I'm stronger, wiser, and more determined than ever to live a life of purpose and joy for myself and my children.

I now work as a Community Health Worker and Recovery Coach in the city where I once felt alone and overpowered. Becoming a

Recovery Coach and Community Health Worker has been one of the most fulfilling experiences of my life. Every time I sit down with someone who's battling their own addiction, I see myself in their eyes. I remember the fear, the doubt, and the hopelessness, but I also remember the moment I realized I could turn it all around. Helping others find that moment for themselves, guiding them through the same storm I weathered, gives me a sense of purpose that I never imagined.

It's more than a job—it's my calling. I always tell myself, "You can put yourself first, heal, pursue your dreams, and start a business." - Aleisha Kuntu

Yolanda Long

Educator - Manetopic by Y-Michelle

Themaneconsultinggroup.com

Yolanda began her career in the beauty industry in 1993, quickly discovering her passion for cosmetology. By 1998, she became a cosmetology educator, sharing her expertise with aspiring beauticians. In 2007, she transitioned into barbering, bringing a fresh perspective to the craft. Her dedication to education continued, and by 2016, she became a barber instructor, empowering the next generation of barbers.

Yolanda holds a master's degree in cosmetology and is a certified Hair Loss Practitioner with an associate degree in Trichology, deepening her knowledge of hair and scalp health. She owned a salon for seven years, blending her practical skills with business acumen. Her commitment to the industry earned her a role as an examiner for the state cosmetology and barber board, ensuring high standards for professionals.

Yolanda's journey reflects her passion for education and her dedication to excellence in the beauty and barbering industry.

The Forever Student: Finding Peace in Endless Learning

By: Yolanda Long

High school was never a place where I felt I belonged. It was a monotonous grind, a series of classes that seemed disconnected from anything meaningful or practical. I was the student who constantly challenged the rules, questioned the relevance of the curriculum, and resisted authority at every turn. Teachers saw me as a troublemaker, a lost cause. I saw myself as a free spirit, unwilling to be confined by the rigid structures of traditional education. My grades were abysmal, and it was nothing short of a miracle that I managed to graduate. The day I walked across the stage to receive my diploma in summer school felt less like a celebration and more like an escape.

With high school behind me, I was confronted with the daunting question of what to do next. College seemed like just another set of shackles, and the idea of entering the workforce with no direction was equally unappealing. I knew I had to find something that resonated with me and felt less like school and more like a calling. That's when I stumbled upon cosmetology.

Cosmetology school offered a singular focus that was immediately appealing. Instead of juggling multiple subjects, I could immerse myself in one craft. The idea of learning to create beauty, to work with my hands, and to connect with people in a tangible way excited me. Enrolling in cosmetology school was a straightforward decision that felt like a breath of fresh air after the suffocating atmosphere of high school.

The environment in cosmetology school was drastically different from what I had known. It was practical, hands-on, and creative. For the first time, I was in a place where I could see the direct application of what I was learning. However, old habits die hard. My rebellious streak and tendency to dismiss details that didn't immediately capture my interest followed me. I struggled to pay attention in class, often missing out on crucial information because I thought I knew better. This attitude turned what should have been a straightforward educational path into a prolonged journey of frustration and self-correction.

Graduating from cosmetology school was a significant milestone, but I quickly realized that holding a license was just the beginning. The world of cosmetology is expansive and ever-changing. The basics I had learned were just the tip of the iceberg. To truly excel, I needed advanced training. This realization was both daunting and humbling. Over the next two years, I dedicated myself to mastering advanced techniques, attending workshops, and learning from seasoned professionals. It was a steep learning curve, but my determination to succeed kept me going. The more I learned, the more I understood the depth and complexity of the field. I regretted not paying more attention during my initial training, but this time around, I was fully committed.

With advanced training under my belt, I felt a sense of accomplishment and confidence in my abilities. My journey, however, didn't end there. The struggles and obstacles I faced ignited a desire to help others who might be on a similar path. I wanted to reach out to students who, like me, were rebellious and resistant to traditional education. Becoming a cosmetology instructor felt like a natural progression. It was a way to channel my experiences into something positive and to give back to a community that had given me so much.

Teaching was a new challenge. Standing in front of a classroom, I saw reflections of my younger self in many of my students. They were bright, creative, and full of potential but also distracted, disinterested, and skeptical of authority. I was only 22 years old and younger than some of my student's children. However, I knew their struggles intimately, and I wanted to help them in a way that traditional education often failed to do. My teaching style was hands-on and engaging. I emphasized the practical aspects of cosmetology, integrating theory in immediately applicable ways. I encouraged my students to experiment, ask questions, and embrace their mistakes. I shared my own stories of failure and success, hoping to show them that the path to mastery is not a straight line but a winding road full of learning opportunities.

Despite being the teacher, I remained a perpetual student. The beauty industry is dynamic, with trends and techniques constantly evolving. I continued attending workshops and advanced courses to stay relevant and effective. This dual role of teacher and student kept me grounded and connected to the ever-changing landscape of cosmetology. It also allowed me to bring fresh insights and cutting-edge knowledge back to my students.

Teaching cosmetology became more than just a job; it was a passion and a mission. Each day, I aimed to inspire my students, help them see their potential, and guide them toward a future where they could succeed on their own terms. I wanted them to understand that being a rebel wasn't inherently bad but that rebellion needed direction and purpose. They could channel their creativity and individuality into a rewarding career through cosmetology.

By my 30s, the career I had once been passionate about began to feel like a never-ending routine. I had been a cosmetologist for years, dedicating myself to mastering the art of beauty. But over time, the spark dimmed. The creative flame that once fueled my work was flickering, and I was burnt out. It was time for a change, something to reignite my passion and give my career a new life. That's when I decided to go back to school—not just any school, but barber college. 2

Returning to barber college in my 30s was both daunting and exhilarating. I was stepping into a new domain that men traditionally dominated and determined to carve out my place in it. The transition from cosmetology to barbering was a challenge, but it also felt like a natural progression. Barbering had its own set of skills and techniques, and learning them required me to push beyond my comfort zone. I was ready to embrace this new chapter with the same rebellious spirit that had defined my younger years.

Barber College was an eye-opener. The atmosphere was different from what I had known in cosmetology school. It was more intense and competitive and required precision and artistry that was both familiar and foreign. I had to learn new techniques, from straight razor shaves to intricate clipper cuts. Each day was a blend of frustration and triumph, but I felt a renewed sense of purpose with each challenge. I was not just learning to cut hair; I was rediscovering my love for the craft.

As a woman in a predominantly male field, I faced my share of skepticism. Some doubted my skills and questioned my place in the barbering world. But these challenges only fueled my determination. I stood my ground, proving myself with each cut, shave, and client who walked out of my chair with a smile. I knew I had to be twice as good to be taken seriously, and embraced that challenge head-on.

After completing my training and earning my barber license, I spent years honing my skills. I built a clientele, earning their trust and respect with my dedication to excellence. The burnout I had felt as a cosmetologist was replaced by a fiery passion for barbering. This new career path was not just a job but a calling.

Nine years into my journey as a barber, I took another significant step—I became a barber instructor. Teaching had always been close to my heart, and becoming an educator in the barbering world felt like coming full circle. As an instructor, I had the opportunity to share my knowledge, experiences, and passion with a new generation of barbers. I was determined to be a mentor and a

role model, especially for the women who, like me, wanted to break into the field.

Standing my ground as a female barber and educator was not always easy. There were moments when I had to assert myself and demand the respect I deserved, but I was unwavering in my commitment. I knew that my presence in the industry was important for me and all the women who aspired to follow this path. I wanted to show them that it was possible to succeed, to be taken seriously, and to excel in a male-dominated field.

As an educator, I emphasized the importance of precision, creativity, and professionalism. I taught my students that barbering was not just about cutting hair but about building relationships, understanding client needs, and continuously improving their craft. I shared my own journey, from the burnout of cosmetology to the rejuvenation of barbering, hoping to inspire them to find their own paths and passions.

My decision to go back to barber college in my 30s was one of the best choices I ever made. It revived my career, reignited my passion, and gave me a new sense of purpose. It also allowed me to break barriers, challenge stereotypes, and make a lasting impact as a female barber and educator. The journey had challenges, but each obstacle made me stronger and more determined.

Looking back, my journey from a rebellious student who barely graduated high school to a dedicated cosmetology and barber instructor was one of transformation and self-discovery. It was about finding my path, embracing my passions, and turning my struggles into strengths. It was about learning to listen, not just to others, but to myself, and realizing that education is not confined to the classroom. Most importantly, it was about understanding that everyone has the potential to succeed if they find the right way to learn and grow.

As I continue to teach and learn, I am reminded daily of the importance of patience, perseverance, and empathy. My students are my mirror, reflecting the challenges I faced and the triumphs I achieved. They inspire me to be better, to learn more, and to teach with a heart full of understanding and a mind open to new possibilities. Through them, I see the future of master barbers and cosmetologists—a bright, diverse, and ever-evolving future, just like the students themselves.

In conclusion, my journey from a high school rebel to a passionate cosmetology and barber instructor has been one of growth, resilience, and continuous learning. It has taught me the value of persistence, the power of focused education, and the importance of giving back. I have learned that every student, no matter how rebellious or resistant, has the potential to achieve greatness with the proper guidance and support. This journey has shaped my career and defined my purpose: to inspire, educate, and transform lives through the art of barber and cosmetology.

Today, I am proud of my accomplishments and the path I've carved for myself. I continue to teach, learn, and grow, always striving to be the best barber and cosmetology instructor I can be. My story is proof of the power of resilience, the importance of following your passion, and the impact one can make by standing their ground and breaking new ground.

Monèl Antut

CEO – BeauNoir

BeauNoir.booksy.com
https://www.facebook.com/mel.long.12
https://www.instagram.com/beaunoir__/

Monèl is dedicated to educating African Americans on the importance of protecting their crown and embracing natural hair. In the spring of 2019, she founded BeauNoir, a safe space where children, women, and men can receive hair maintenance, repair, and styling. BeauNoir represents Black beauty, self-love, strength, and courage.

Born and raised in Madison, WI, Monèl is the first entrepreneur in her family. In her free time, she enjoys practicing yoga, meditation, and hiking. A lover of expression, especially through poetry, Monel chose to write her chapter in poems, reflecting her passion for creativity and self-discovery.

The Crown We Wear: A Story of Self-Love and Resilience

By Monèl Antut

As a kid, I made my siblings play school throughout the week. I would create a schedule for the day and teach them numbers, letters, and different worksheets to strengthen their math skills. I naturally gravitated towards teaching, nurturing, and aiding in any way, shape, or form that fit at the time.

As a young child, it didn't dawn on me that I was actually stepping into my true life purpose. I was the light when we experienced hardship. Regardless of how I felt, I managed to put them before me and sacrificed my childhood to make sure theirs was full of good moments. No one told me to do this. I just knew my role and took action when the opportunity presented itself. I committed myself to being the peace and harmony in my household.

I would wake up early in the mornings and make my younger brother bottles and prepare a slight breakfast for all of us. I would find matching outfits since there were 5 of us, and we all dressed in similar colors. I figured it made it easier for moma. I don't recall ever having a good night's rest as a child. I often checked my siblings' breathing while they rested and listened out till moma got home. I wondered why I was the one who took the role of an adult, even though I was just a child.

I'm not going to lie, it is quite lonely not having any sisters. I couldn't really connect with my brothers and tell them about boys I had crushes on or even about having a period. I would journal a lot; that's where I kept all my secrets. I would find myself writing poems when I wasn't creating raps. I enjoyed expressing myself through my entries, but I also discovered that I lost my voice in the same process.

I felt that my opinion didn't matter, and when I did try to speak up, I was told the famous saying, 'Stay in a child's place.' I had to find some sort of fun outlet while growing up, especially since I was the only girl. I took it upon myself to do my brother's hair and mine. I believe that is when I first fell in love with natural hair. I tried different conditioners, oils, and gels till I figured out what worked the best.

Before I knew it, I was a family hairstylist, ranging from twists, clipping ends, and straightening hair to crinkles.

BeauNoir means Black Beauty; I take pride in my natural hair business and the root meaning. We often take for granted what we have, not realizing that everything we have is perfect. Many of us are out of touch with our roots and out of alignment with our higher self. There are center points in our body that store energy, and I want to teach you about one specific placement called the *Muladhara*. This is the root chakra. The root chakra is the root foundation where life energy is stored. It attaches our physical and spiritual to this plane, allowing us to be grounded.

Muladhara is associated with the earth element; it's like a safety net full of security, balance, and stability. When you practice alignment with the *Muladhara*, you have access to move that energy freely throughout your body and gain a higher sense of self/self-worth. My clients who have decided to embrace their natural hair and start their loc journey have also begun working on their *Muladhara*.
Each of my clients has different hair textures, different journeys, and different passions. Each year with locs, you reach a new milestone in your life. Locs are like a soulmate; they are always by your side and hold you accountable for all your actions. They know when you are loving yourself because it shows in the way that you love them. They show you what is going on internally, and you have to have those hard conversations with your stylist and be truthful about what is going on in your life.

I love the relationship and spiritual connection between locs and self. When you start your loc journey, you are committing yourself to a higher lifestyle with a whole new set of beliefs. It's a slow process of transformation, and it can't be rushed. The process of caring for locs represents a spiritual practice that involves caring for self. Locs need nourishment, care, and consistency. This journey will test your devotion and commitment to change and grow.

I wanted to learn how to make African Americans embrace their natural beauty and become comfortable within themselves. In my words, the spiritual meaning of locs is divine connection to the eternal source of life, as above, so below. We come from an abundance of love, wisdom, and strength. Locs are protecting our crown chakra, representing the universal consciousness we all share.

I hope one of my poems connects with my readers on a deeper level and helps you gain a deeper understanding of entrepreneurship in the beauty industry.

I see you

I see you
Long, thick, and tangled

I feel you
Coils, twist, and wavy

I hear you
Water, sunlight, and rainbows

I am you
Happy, sad, and thankful

My pride is anchored in my hair; it knows everything about me.
We operate in sync, and there's a healthy balance in my hair care.
We complement one another day in and day out.

I pour water, and she sprouts.
I massage my scalp, and she grows by the second.
I give her vitamin E, Shea butter, and aloe, and she thanks me every

morning when she wakes me up with hair hugs full of love.

I see you

Welcoming Deandrae T.

My breasts are tender

My back hurts

Knees weak

I can't work

My chest tightens

Gasping for air

Calling 911, someone get him out of here

My feet are soaked

I'm screaming in fear

My child is born in 2020

Into a world full of fear

COVID-19 was really my worst nightmare

No guidance

No support

Tears falling for Larry Green

The only dad I ever knew

Passed before he met you

Today, I choose to wipe my eyes

& chase my dream because of you

My son will always know I chose to create a life of happiness

All while pursuing my dream to be a creator

Pursuing A Better Version of Me

Books piling up through the roof

The curriculum is really outrageous

How do I tell my professor that I cannot create a schedule

That gives me enough time to complete all these assignments?

I'd rather just tell 'em, "Yo, you bugging."

I'm working around the clock, doubles back to back.
Shoe boxes stacked with racks
Somehow, none of it matters.
Money never meant much to me, and I'd rather have genuine company.
Real connections come with valuable lessons; let me teach one.

Throw away any advice that taught you to silence your creativity.
Use the tool of silence, and you'll hear me.

Message to Lynett

My palms are moist

My legs are shaking

The skin on the back of my neck is standing up

I could hear a penny drop

There are five people ahead of me

I would pull my hair out rather than present this speech

I hear my soul speak to me, "Calm down and breathe, mama, you got this. You know you were born to speak."

I believed every word I heard, and before I could get myself together, I heard my instructor on the speaker,

"Please give a warm welcome to Monel Antut."

The crowd erupted in cheer.

Inhale

Exhale

Everything around me stopped—the sounds, the cheers, the hairs slowly went back into their natural placement.

I froze time, and I saw a girl with big eyes looking right at me.

My 5-year-old mothering childhood self was there, watching me.

I froze for a moment, not sure what to say to her.

I asked her, "Is she ok? Does she want to talk?"

She smiled and said, "No talks, just hugs today."

We cried and hugged for what seemed like a lifetime.

She told me, "Let them hear our words and heal from our words,"

and within a second, she was gone.

I gave them my rawest form; that was the day a healed version of

myself was born.

12.27.

Kujichagulia - Self-Determination
Stand tall
Step into your power
You are the flesh and blood of your
Ancestors.
Everything you do is in honor of them.

Make choices through faith.
See without sight
Create without vision
Activate your intuition
You are everything
And also nothing at all.

Don't get caught up in what you can
see. Hence, we only see through flaws.

Throughout my journey, I've learned that self-determination is not just about pushing through life's challenges but about embracing who you are, where you come from, and the path that you're destined to walk. From nurturing my siblings as a child to guiding others on their loc journey, I've always been drawn to helping others find their own sense of power and alignment.

BeauNoir is more than a business to me... It's a reflection of my own growth and the wisdom I've gained along the way. I hope that my story and the lessons I've shared help you find the courage to stand tall in your own power, to honor your roots, and to create a life that aligns with your higher self. You are everything and also nothing at all—don't get caught up in the surface. Look deeper, and you'll see the beauty that lies within.

Kiauna Montgomery

CEO Simple Cuts Plus

https://www.facebook.com/kiauna.montgomery
Simplecutssalon.booksy.com

Kiauna is a dedicated mother, sister, and friend who finds immense joy in nurturing her family and creating beautiful memories together. Her passion for doing hair is more than just a hobby—it's an art form that allows her to express her creativity while helping others feel confident and beautiful. Whether she's styling a new look or offering a listening ear, Kiauna takes pride in being there for her loved ones.

Balancing her roles, Kiauna ensures that her family feels supported and cherished every day. Her journey as a mother has taught her patience, resilience, and the true meaning of unconditional love. As a sister and friend, she strives to be a source of strength and positivity. Kiauna's life is a blend of love, creativity, and dedication, and she wouldn't have it any other way. Each day, she embraces the opportunity to care for her family and pursue her passion for hair, finding fulfillment in both.

My Testimony: My Portrait

By: Kiauna Montgomery

This is my story. My name is Kiauna. I am 37 years old and a mother of 3 beautiful children, ages 21, 13, and 8, and soon to be a grandmother of a little baby boy.

Just a short background: I became a mother at the age of 15. I didn't know what my passion in life was or would become, but as a young girl, I have always been a nurturer, caregiver, and overall just a loving person. At such a young age, I didn't understand how big of a factor this would play in my life.

I have been a licensed cosmetologist for 13 years, but my life changed completely 10 years ago. After working for my boss at the salon for 2 years with no pay raise, I ended up finding a night job as a second income to support my family. I did this for a year until it became unbearable, so I decided I needed to ask for a raise or leave the salon.

Being at the salon for 2+ years, I developed a best friend who I always consulted with, especially when making life-changing decisions. I asked her if she would go with me to talk to him because I was scared to go alone, and she said, "Of course I will go with you, Kiauna. You deserve a raise; you do more than enough."

She walked in with me, and we sat down to talk. I asked for a raise and told him if not, I would be looking to leave. He looked at both of us and said, "To be honest, I no longer want the salon. If you both want to buy it, it's yours." I looked at her, she looked at me, and I said, "You want to?" She replied, "You want to?"

In 2014, we bought the salon. I became a salon owner at 27 years old. I had no idea what I was getting into, seeing as this was my first business, but I felt comfortable doing it with my best friend and now business partner.

As I thought my life was changing upward as a mother, stylist, and business owner, in 2015, I got the biggest blow of my life. I received a phone call from my mother, which I didn't know would be the last conversation I'd ever have with her. That day, my life and roles completely changed. After talking to my mother and her expressing that she couldn't breathe, I told her to call the ambulance. The next phone call was from her boyfriend, telling me they said her heart stopped.

I had made a promise to my mother that I would take care of her babies (my younger sister and brother) if anything ever happened to her. She used to make me promise this, though I didn't fully understand why at the time. Three days later, after she passed, I found out I was pregnant with my now 8-year-old daughter.

Now I'm 27, going on 28, already a mother of 2, but now becoming a mother of 5. I still had to work, pour into my clients, and then come home and pour into my family, while dealing with grief (which I didn't know how to handle for myself, but could do for others). Now, at 28 years old and pregnant, I had to care for a 16-year-old, 14-year-old, 12-year-old, and 4-year-old, while learning to manage everything that came with it.

Five years later, COVID-19 hit, the world shut down, there was no work, no school, and everyone was wearing masks. Life completely changed. I continued therapy, healing, and then found out I was suffering from anxiety. Through this process, I never got to truly focus on Kiauna. I couldn't fully express what I needed or wanted. All I knew was that I made a promise to my mother to take care of her babies and my babies, and I was determined to do whatever that entailed.

I started therapy and began healing from everything—trauma and grief behind the chair. My biggest support came from my best friend and business partner, who has stood by me for the past 10 years. No matter how many times I wanted to quit, she wouldn't let me. From taking me to church to signing me up for various business endeavors to keep me busy, she was the biggest blessing to me and my family.

As we returned to work in person, I reconnected with my amazing clients, who also helped me more than they will ever know. This love and therapy helped me grow and thrive as a successful barber/stylist.

Now here we are in June 2024, with the opening of a brand-new, expanded salon. What I thought was going to break me has become my biggest strength as a businesswoman, mother, friend, and partner. As I continue to heal, grow, and thrive in my purpose, I've come to understand that my purpose is greater than me. But I will continue to thrive in it.

Through all the ups and downs, I've learned that life's challenges don't break you—they shape you. Losing my mother, raising my siblings and children, and managing a business wasn't easy, but it has made me stronger in ways I never imagined. To other women facing hardships, remember: don't be afraid to lean on the people who love you, and trust in your own strength. You don't have to do everything alone—ask for help when you need it, and surround yourself with supportive people.

Opening this new, expanded salon is more than just a business accomplishment—it's a symbol of everything I've survived and everything I've grown into. So even when things feel overwhelming, take it one step at a time and know that each struggle is preparing you for something greater. My purpose is bigger than me, and I will continue to walk in it, no matter the obstacles. For any woman chasing her dreams: keep going, even when it's tough. Believe in yourself, and know that every challenge is a chance to grow. Through pain and grief came my strength and humility, and through this test, I found my testimony. I am her, and she is me—Kiauna

Sherronda Booker

Owner Operator of Sherronda's Home Hair

https://www.facebook.com/sherronda1
https://www.instagram.com/sherronda30

Sherronda Booker is a 44-year-old mother of three whose goal is to create a legacy of honor, hard work, and dedication to family and community. Raised on the South Side of Chicago in a loud, proud, and boisterous family, she grew into her voice after realizing that life's trials and tribulations are stepping stones and learning lessons.

By creatively navigating these challenges, she believes they can propel you to new heights. Through her journey, Sherronda hopes to inspire women to recognize their strengths and use them to positively impact their families and, ultimately, the world.

From Paralysis To Progress A Star Is Born: Nebula In The Beginning

By: Sherronda Booker

I've realized that my foundation in resiliency was laid during the early years of my life—almost as if I were born resilient. I believe I was! In fact, I know I was.

6944 S. Justine is the house I was born in. I remember warm winter mornings of having Kool-Aid and cheese slices with my brother and the wonking of the Atari as he collected Pac-Man points. Like most African American women, I was born into a family that had to overcome some pretty rough obstacles—the ones designed to dismantle the Black family. Yet, in this environment, my foundation of resilience, being able to bounce back from anything, was firmly laid, shaping me into the person I am today.

I had my mom, dad, and a brother who was seven years older than me. My mother was going to Kennedy King Community College to obtain her Associate's degree, the same path I took 20 years later. There is a story of where she had to come to get a 2-year-old me because my father was being arrested for back child support for my half-brother. I remember feeling sad and confused, watching him from our front room window get into what I thought was a cab and leave me behind. He was actually getting into a police car– how the young mind paints its own picture.

As a young child, I was close to my dad. My father worked late nights to support his family, and I would stay up late nights waiting for him to come home. We would eat the room-temperature dinner my mom would leave for him on the stove.

When I was around five years old, due to my father's drug use, we lost our home and our white picket fence. Despite all the bad things associated with living there, that optimism of resiliency still leaves me with fond memories of living in my childhood home. It was a home. From my perspective, we were the picture-perfect family. I had my mom, who was attending school to better her future, a dad who worked hard to provide for his family, and an older brother. My foundation of resiliency was being laid.

Stardust

When we lost our white picket fence, we had to move in with my mother's side of the family. My mother's side of the family has an exciting history. My grandparents moved to Chicago in the 1940s because my grandfather, Willie TBo Booker, ran into some kind of trouble in his hometown of Chickasaw, Mississippi. He came first and slowly began to send for my grandmother and his siblings and cousins. My grandfather was an entrepreneur who ran several businesses to support his family. I come from a resilient people. I didn't get a chance to meet him or my grandmother, but their offspring raised me, and I have fond memories of them, solidifying that they were telling the truth by saying, "On Ada and Daddy, I ain't lying."

It was an adventure for me to be living with my aunts, uncles, and cousins. It was always a circus with people coming and going. Friends of the family staying the night, strangers knocking at the door at all times of the night. Our holiday parties were the best. Everyone would add something to make it all come together. Thanksgiving, Christmas, and even our Halloween parties were full of family and friends. It was the era of Michael Jackson's *Billie Jean*, Prince's *Purple Rain*, and Spike Lee's *Skool Dayz*.

However, I did experience my first police raid after moving in with them, an unsettling introduction to the realities of my family's involvement in drug sales. It wasn't the only raid I would be in. I remember being scared and confused, not knowing what was going on.

I felt like that a lot during those days. It was the beginning of puberty for me. Plus, my mom's youngest brother battled an addiction to PCP, and when he succumbed to AIDS in 1992, my family again showed their resilience as they came together to provide care for him during his time in hospice.

All the while, I was co-captain of the Fulton Falcon Elementary cheer team and danced on stage with M.C. Hammer at one of his concerts. I also went on my first and only overnight camping trip. Each of those moments and countless others have significantly impacted my future in leadership.

I always took advantage of my opportunities, no matter the circumstances. Another testament of resiliency!

Protostar: Living Off Xperience

I can remember learning that I was an introvert around 11 or 12. Knowing that has helped me a lot in my adulthood. I've learned that I like to engage with people and have a good time, but I can only spend so much time on it. I exchange a lot of energy with people; then, I want to go home to retreat and recover.

As a child, I loved hanging out with my friends, playing video games, and forming dance groups. However, I would sometimes have my family tell my friends I was asleep because I would rather stay inside watching television and eat the snacks my mom would buy me rather than hang out outside. That was my special time and my happy place. I often say that television raised me. Television allowed me to travel to different places and see how other people lived, all from the comfort of my home. Television also helped me escape some of the harsh realities of that same home.

I was around the age of 11 or 12 when I was the victim of my first sexual assault. A cousin's friend whom we had "adopted" because his mom had passed, an older teen, who had been living with us for at least 4 or 5 years, had the nerve to lift my nightgown while I was sleeping, lying on my stomach, and gaze at my underaged butt. I woke up in a foggy state, not quite sure if that was what had happened. Being scared and confused, I only confided in my best friend. Then he did something similar to her, and she told her mom, who then went to tell my mom.

When my mom found out, she was pissed. She beat him with an old table leg she picked up on the way home from the candy store, where she found me to ask if he had touched me. He was arrested but soon released. Since he was an orphan, he was allowed to move back into my family's house. I had to cohabit with my molester until I was around 13 or 14 years old. That was a big test of me being resilient.

The second sexual assault occurred when I was 14 years old–a stranger this time. I was on my way home from my first-year of high school's orientation. I was feeling all proud. I was taking the bus home, trying to figure out the best route for when school started. I had just made it to the corner of my block when some random guy came up to me and put his arm around my neck like he was trying to talk to me, you know, get my number or something. I got from under his arm like, "Nah, I'm cool." Then again, he put his arm around my neck, but this time, he added pressure like a chokehold and told me I was about to go with him. I was afraid and talked to God the whole time. He walked me several blocks past my house. We went past people I knew, but I was too scared to ask for help because he had threatened me, saying he had a gun. We finally ended up at an abandoned building right down the street from my home.
My instincts kicked in to tell him that I was on my period. That caused him to jump up and run away, leaving me to count to 10 before I got up.

That experience made me feel like I had to start to protect myself. I gained my south side of Chicago's tough girl side. My childhood helped me become who I am now: one of the most positive, optimistic, brightest lights you'll ever meet. It seems that is because I've always been able to identify and focus on the positives by acknowledging the trauma but not living in it. Yes, these things happened to me, but they don't define me.
I am a rape victim, not a victim to rape.
I choose to live, rather than wallow in misery.

I Can See The Stars With I.C.Stars

Close to my 40th birthday, while I was juggling motherhood to a high school junior, plus a 6th and 2nd grader, I had received my

Associate's degree and gotten a cosmetology license. I ended up volunteering (which turned into working) at my kid's school when Covid came, and we were quarantined. "The Great Quarantine" is what they will call it. With everyone stuck inside our homes, I, like most moms, was looking for activities for the children to stay busy. I found a virtual coding and financial literacy program for my 11-year-old son. Every day, I would remind him to ensure he was logged on and completing the assignments, like a mom.

One day, while scrolling social media, I stumbled upon a tech program for adults, i.c.stars. The next cycle was starting soon, so I decided to at least look into it.

When I attended the information session that explained precisely how the program would go, I saw that my resiliency was about to be tested. The program consists of 12-hour days, five days a week, with a $200 weekly stipend for four months. I would learn how to build a website while developing business and leadership skills. I would have to work 12-hour days, virtually, while helping three remote students get used to learning online.

I had to go through a rigorous application process and an exciting panel interview before landing my spot in Cycle 47. Once the program began, I had to get to know 20 new people, their personalities, and their working styles because I had to work with them to achieve the same goal. I was learning new coding languages, which was like learning a new language. Ultimately, I had to learn exactly what I was made of.

From the start of the program, I was shown that everything I had overcome from childhood until then had made me resilient. During the 16 weeks of the program, I was pushed to limits I never thought I would encounter, let alone overcome. With each task I completed, I knew the next was close behind, so I would celebrate that victory and prepare to face the next one.

From then on, I approached life from the viewpoint that whatever I would come up against, I would figure out a way to solve it. The program "programmed" me to bring out my troubleshooting capabilities. I learned to become creative when I came up against "salt blocks." I stopped referring to them as "roadblocks" because I learned we can chip away at salt blocks. If we take time to figure it out, stay the course, and remain resilient, we can get through most things.

I've had the honor and pleasure of working for i.c.stars for the past year as the Candidate Assessment Associate. I help new stars find their way into the galaxy by hosting informational sessions about the program for potential candidates and assisting applicants through the application process—reciprocity at its finest.

The Blackhole: A Journey of Resilience

After four months, I commenced the program. I had the honor of being an organizing director for the Black Cornerstones project. By chance, I was hired by a Black woman, making the most money I'd ever made while learning how to mobilize my community by channeling people, funds, and resources. I met her during a virtual forum she hosted to combat the recent carjackings our neighborhood was facing. I invited her to witness the community building at i.c.stars, and from that moment on, she gave me her trust.

For three intense months, I immersed myself in collecting the lived experiences of family and friends through recorded conversations on how life was when they grew up in their neighborhoods. It was exciting hearing different people talk about fond memories from their childhoods. I wanted to capture the experiences that most of our children will never get to witness. I proudly organized street clean-ups and hosted gatherings in the community garden to help foster community engagement. I even orchestrated a motorcade for The John Lewis Day Of Action. It was a day that encouraged voting by having motorcades (a parade of cars) leaving from sites throughout the city to gather at one meeting place.

That role helped cultivate my organizing skills and improve my leadership capabilities. I also learned to celebrate my mistakes because there is always something to learn from.

When my contract ended, I started my corporate technical apprenticeship—a five-month fellowship. I had to learn the ins and outs of each product at this new company by earning certifications and passing a test at the end of the five months. The apprenticeship ended, and I landed a role in recruitment. Working in human resources was ideal for me because of my personality type. I enjoy engaging with people. One of my mentors said, "I would be bringing the 'Human' back to HR."

That job came with plenty of perks: a remote work environment, a personalized office setup that was FedExed to my home, and a paycheck that made some of my family members envy me.

The last challenge was, and still is, the most difficult: having to be resilient and face life head-on, all while blocking out the negative energy, thoughts, and feelings of the people whom I considered close. These were the same people I ultimately wanted to share the gifts of a more lucrative career with—the opportunity to build a life of luxury and leisure.

I had to stay steadfast in what I knew was right for me, even while having "loved ones" in my ear telling me I couldn't do it, despite them seeing me doing it. That was the greatest test of my resiliency—drowning out the naysayers who, at one point, had so much of my ear, and listening to my own voice, believing in MY self, MY mind, MY strengths, and MY capabilities.

Also, I practiced patience and gave myself grace to recognize when and where I fell short and to ask for help in those areas, because we can't do it all by ourselves. It does take a village, but you must first identify who you are as a person to recognize who your village is. You are not always born into yours. Remember, villages matter, and most times, you must build your own.

The Essence of Me - My Heritage

I am a Booker-Love woman. My mother, Bonnie Booker, was born the youngest daughter of 9 siblings and a twin. Her parents raised her until her early teens, when she lost her mother, my grandmother, Ada

Below-Booker, at the tender age of 16. That was the same year my mom gave birth to my brother. She lost her dad the very next year when she was a 17-year-old single mother. I get my resiliency from her, no doubt.

My mom's side of the family is composed of some very strong women. They are the ones who provided a clear vision for me to see how women lead. I can remember thinking only women had jobs because the women in my family got up and went to work every day. The men in my family—my brother, male cousins, and most of my uncles—stayed home and hustled.

I get the Love in me from my dad's side of the family. His mom, Ms. Roz Love, was the only grandmother I've known while she was alive. We had a great relationship in her later years, always talking on the phone. She was a spunky woman who had taken my aunts and moved to Florida when I was around 6 or 7. Like my mother, she lost her mom at a young age—she was only 9.

Some of the last things my grandma told me before she passed at the age of 92 were, "To keep a stiff upper lip," which I interpret to mean to tell my story with truth and dignity, and not to let anyone else tell it for me.

My Inspirational Board of Directors

I can remember watching "The Oprah Winfrey" show around the age of 12. The topic of the show centered on women turning 40 years old. They discussed how freeing it was once they reached the age of 40. It was like they had found a new "joy" that, at the young age of 11 or 12 years old, I was eager to reach 40.

When I turned 40, I was part of i.c.stars, surrounded by powerful women. Our program manager made sure we stayed on point. She did her job very well and inspired me to be great during the process.

At that time, the organization's CEO was a powerful woman who showed me that leadership could be displayed on many different levels. It was not always loud and boisterous like I had seen in the past.

Our Resident Counselor, my adjunct spiritual advisor, showed me how to go inside myself to find everything I needed. She led group "breathing" exercises and taught me how to use my imagination more creatively to bring joy into my life.

Then there was my cyclemate, the Scrum Master on our team. She constantly reminded me that, in most instances, I was right in my thinking while I constantly doubted myself. I also had my business partner and friend around. She told me I needed to consider my worth when seeking roles and looking at salaries. She also instilled in me not to have imposter syndrome. She is a proud Aquarius who consistently shows me that I belong in every room I enter!

They were my Board of Directors, coaches, and mentors through some of my toughest times, reminding me of who I was before I could trigger that in myself. It was a constant battle of having to remember who I am: a wise, strong, intelligent Black woman who had, could, and would stand the test of time with each test I faced. I chose not to worry about the past or have anxiety about the future. I decided to focus on what was in front of me while it was in front of me.

Reflecting on where I am after 44 years, I am a licensed cosmetologist who travels to senior clients to offer services; some of my clients are bedridden. I own a Cleaning and Lawn Care service, There's A Rose, which will be my family's legacy business. I also work from 9 to 5 as a recruiter for a top non-profit business, leadership, technology, and workforce development program in Chicago. All the while, I've helped cultivate my community by sitting on the Board of Directors of a community garden and as the Vice-President of the Parent Council at my children's African-centered charter school.

My Why

When it comes to being resilient and staying the course, it is best to focus on the reasons you are doing whatever you're doing. I call this "remembering my why."

My children are my why, like most mothers. They are why I endure, go through, put up with, conquer, face, fail, and try again and again. There is a line in this song that says, "I got a really big team, and they want some really big things," and I know they deserve some really big rings, so I have no other choice but to do my thing.

I remember trying to teach my youngest son how to count coins using one of those books you get from Walmart that shows pictures of the coins and other colorful math lessons. He looked me straight in the eyes and said, "Mom, we're going to be counting millions, not pennies!"

I have a mission to fulfill. When I decided to bring them into this world, I made a commitment to God to provide them with all the things they need to ensure they have a happy, healthy childhood. I believe that when children have the stability of a solid foundation by having a safe environment to grow, just like a plant, they will blossom into constructive, proactive citizens who give back to the world.

Being resilient means not giving up. It means pausing to reflect but continuing until the puzzle has been solved. It means not having any other choice but to make a way.

Resiliency is a mindset. You have to believe that you can keep going, that you can push through. You have to keep a focused mind.

It's Bigger Than Me

I wanted to be a part of this book journey to inspire others to be the light.

I want to shine so bright that my children look at me with no worries or fears because they know with me, everything will be alright. I want the warmth of my shine to comfort them.

I greet people with "Happy Monday" or whatever day of the week it is, whether in person, through text message, or via email, because I want to remind people that life is not all that serious. If it is, then eventually, like always, everything will work itself out and be alright.

We have to take life one day at a time. Some days, I am taking things one minute at a time. I ensure I am not getting too overwhelmed with life's instances by chipping away at one thing as I go along.

I also engage in self-care and indulge in things that make me happy. I practice yoga with friends, dance to House music, and get massages often to get rid of the toxins in my body. I pay attention to my body and give it what it needs.

Spending time with my children is one of my most favorite pastimes. It takes me back to my childhood. I get to have just as much fun as they are having. Now, that releases so much stress! Ultimately, I try to overcome one obstacle at a time.

On The UP side

As I move forward into this next stage of life, I am filled with excitement and optimism. This chapter of my journey has been about embracing my true self, celebrating my resilience, and reaffirming my inner strength. Through telling my story in this book, I've had the opportunity to reflect on the trials I've faced, the lessons I've learned, and the woman I've become. I am uncovering new parts of myself every day, and it's been a liberating experience. The future is bright, and no matter what comes my way, I know I am ready to face it with courage and grace. I am strong, I am prepared, and most of all, I am resilient!

Final tidbit:

I intend to spread peace, love, and hope by reminding people that just because we live in trauma doesn't mean we have to sit in it. To all the women reading this, remember that no matter what trauma or challenges you've faced, you don't have to stay stuck in them. Life can be overwhelming, but you have the power to choose how you respond. Self-care is essential, whether it's through exercise, meditation, or spending time doing what you love, make it a priority. Every challenge you face builds your resilience, so acknowledge the tough times, but don't let them define you. Surround yourself with positive, supportive people who lift you up; you may not always be born into a supportive village, but you can build one by carefully choosing those who empower you. When life feels overwhelming, take it one day at a time, breaking things into smaller, manageable steps, slow progress is still progress. Always remember your "why" whether it's for your family, your dreams, or your own personal growth. Let that be the force that keeps you going. You are powerful, capable, and deserving of joy. Spread love, peace, and hope! Just because you've experienced pain doesn't mean you have to stay in it.

You have the strength to rise above it and live a life of fulfillment. - Sherronda Booker

Kathy Rivers

Owner - Seasoned Just Right Catering

https://www.linkedin.com/in/k-rivers-approach-67129919a/
https://www.instagram.com/approaching_coaching/

Kathy Rivers is the author of "From Trauma to True Me," a transformative work focused on healing and self-discovery. She has 28 years of experience as a hairstylist and 5 years as the owner of Seasoned Just Right Catering.

Beyond her entrepreneurial achievements, Kathy is a dedicated pastor, providing spiritual guidance and support. She is also a loving mother, wife, and proud Yaya, deeply cherishing her family while balancing her professional and spiritual callings.

Reclaiming your Strength and Wholeness

By: Kathy Rivers

With over 28 years of experience as a stylist, one important lesson I've learned is that we all possess inner strength. Sometimes that inner strength is suppressed. When we make up our minds, the strength from within helps guide us toward completeness and wholeness. Doing hair from behind the chair, I've grown in the skill of listening, even over the blow dryer. After people relax and get their hair done, enjoy a good shampoo, their confidence rises, and a sense of inner strength emerges. The saying of, when you look good you feel good!

Every person has a unique strength, often untapped and waiting to be realized. It all starts with a mindset shift—deciding that you're worthy and that you can rise above whatever challenges you face. Once you choose to move forward, that inner strength begins to show itself, helping you navigate obstacles you once thought were insurmountable. This is the foundation of personal growth and transformation.

Wholeness isn't achieved overnight, nor is it a destination you arrive at. It's a continuous journey of recognizing your worth and finding balance in your life. By tapping into your inner strength, you align with your true purpose. Along the way, there may be struggles and setbacks, but those moments truly shape you. They build resilience; with each step, you become more empowered, learning to trust yourself and your capabilities.

When motivating yourself and others to reach wholeness, it's important to recognize that the mind is a powerful tool. Positive change starts with how you think about yourself and your potential. Once you embrace that mindset, you're not just on the road to personal strength—you're on the path to becoming the best version of yourself.
I understand deeply what it feels like to not feel whole or complete while healing from past traumas. I masked my emotions by looking

good on the outside. When on the inside what I have been through had tried to define who I was. I share my story so that others may be healed and encouraged. I thought I would never rise above the constant mental anguish of how I felt about myself. I've experienced being kidnapped, family incest, and violated by numerous men from the age of 4 to 12 years old. I'll be on a whole novel if I talk about the effects of breaking and conquering rejection. But God reminded me that healing and restoration are possible through Him. In NIV Psalm 147:3, we are reminded, "He heals the brokenhearted and binds up their wounds." No matter the depth of our pain, God's love has the power to restore every part of us that feels shattered.

For me, healing was not something I knew how to look for. I thought healing looked like not becoming addicted like my mom. (she recovered today with an amazing testimony). I thought it looked like making sure I had all my children by the one man I married and protecting my children by working hard to give us a better life than I had. Being at the top of my industry I found that none of that mattered, and it wasn't the escape to being free. My mind was bound by fear, self-sabotage, imposter syndrome , low self-esteem, people-pleasing, and afraid of speaking up for myself.

Healing is a journey, and it's important to remember that God is with us every step of the way. In Isaiah 43:2, the Lord promises, "When you pass through the waters, I will be with you; and when you pass through the rivers, they will not sweep over you." Even when it feels like we are drowning in our past hurts, God walks with us, carrying us toward wholeness.
I had to be made new (2 Corinthians 5:17). No trauma can define us, and no brokenness is too great for His grace to repair. In God, you can find true peace and a renewed sense of completeness, knowing He works all things for good (Romans 8:28). Keep trusting in His power, and He will make you whole again.
Reclaiming strength after trauma is a deeply personal exploration, but it's possible to find healing and resilience through faith, self-reflection, plenty of therapy and action. Here are some steps to help you reclaim your strength.
Start by leaning on your faith. In times of trauma, there is a place where you feel alone or no one understands. You find the greatest

place of strength in those kinds of places. My grandmother called it being in between a rock and a hard place. God can be our greatest source of strength and comfort. Philippians 4:13 reminds us, "I can do all things through Christ who strengthens me." Consistent praying, reading scripture, and trusting in God's promises can give you the inner strength to overcome what you've been through. Remember, He is close to the brokenhearted and saves those who are crushed in spirit (Psalm 34:18).

To reclaim strength, it's important to acknowledge and accept the pain you've experienced. Ignoring trauma only delays healing. Instead, allow yourself to feel and process the emotions tied to the experience. This is not a sign of weakness but of strength. As Psalm 30:5 reminds us, "Weeping may endure for a night, but joy comes in the morning."
Forgiving and learning to let go. Holding on to anger, resentment, or guilt can drain your strength. Forgiveness doesn't mean forgetting, but it frees you from being bound by the pain. I was taunted by the memories of the pain and wondered why I was protected more as a child. Did I have a target on my back that said, abuse me? There is a way of forgiving and letting God and its okay to acknowledge that I was wounded. Forgiving was hard for me. It was learning to trust others that wasn't out to abuse and that simply wanted to love me for me.

Ephesians 4:31-32 encourages us to let go of bitterness and anger and forgive others, just as God has forgiven us. Through forgiveness, you reclaim your power and break free from the emotional chains that trauma may have placed on you. We do not have to be imprisoned in our minds. Today I'm so sure and confident in the woman I have become. Because of what I have overcome,I am deeply passionate about empowering women and youth to embrace confidence in their true inner selves.
Having a good support system is helpful when it comes to healing the voice within. You are not meant to go through the healing process alone. Seek out a community of support through trusted friends, family, a therapist, or a faith-based group. Ecclesiastes 4:9-10 tells us, " Two are better than one...if either of them falls, one can

help the other up." Surround yourself with people who uplift and encourage you in your journey toward reclaiming strength.

Trauma can distort how you view yourself, leaving you feeling weak or broken. But Romans 12:2 tells us to "be transformed by the renewing of your mind." Fill your mind with positive affirmations, scriptural truths, and healing thoughts. Focus on your identity as a beloved child of God, whole and strong in Him.

Healing is not linear—it's a journey with ups and downs. Give yourself grace and patience as you navigate this process. Isaiah 40:31 encourages us: "But those who hope in the Lord will renew their strength. They will soar on wings like eagles." Trust that, with time and God's guidance, you will reclaim your strength and rise above your past.

By anchoring yourself in God's love and promises, surrounding yourself with support, and embracing your journey, you can reclaim the strength that trauma tried to take from you.
Finding your voice from within is an empowering journey of self-discovery and authenticity. It involves connecting with your true self, embracing your unique strengths, and confidently expressing your thoughts and values. Here are some steps to help you find your inner voice.
Before you can find your voice, you need to fully understand who you are. Psalm 139:14 reminds us that we are "fearfully and wonderfully made." Reflect on what makes you unique—your experiences, beliefs, passions, and values. Recognize that your voice is tied to your identity, and God has given you a purpose that only you can fulfill.
Often, we silence our inner voice due to doubt, fear, or external influences. You need to start listening to your thoughts, feelings, and instincts to reclaim it. Spend time in prayer or meditation, asking God to reveal your true desires and purpose. Proverbs 3:5-6 encourages us to "trust in the Lord with all your heart" and lean not on our understanding. You'll hear your voice more clearly as you quiet the noise around you.

We often struggle to speak up because we fear how others perceive us. But finding your voice requires courage and a willingness to be vulnerable. Galatians 1:10 reminds us that we're not here to please people but to serve Christ. When you stop seeking approval from others, you free yourself to express your true thoughts and feelings without fear.

Finding your voice isn't about speaking loudly; it's about speaking authentically and confidently. Start small by expressing your opinions in safe environments, such as with trusted friends or a faith group. As you gain confidence, you'll be able to articulate your thoughts and beliefs more freely. Remember 2 Timothy 1:7: "For God has not given us a spirit of fear but of power and love and a sound mind."

Your inner voice may be silenced by self-doubt or criticism. Be kind to yourself and allow room for growth and mistakes. Philippians 4:13 reminds us, "I can do all things through Christ who strengthens me." Embrace the idea that your voice is valid and needed, even when it's not perfect. God strengthens you, and His grace covers your imperfections.

Your voice has power when used with intention. Whether you advocate for yourself, share your beliefs, or encourage others, your voice carries meaning. 1 Peter 4:10 says, "Each of you should use whatever gift you have received to serve others." Know that your words can inspire, heal, and uplift when used with purpose. Let your voice be a reflection of your freedom! Let your voice be shaped by God's truth, allowing Him to direct your words.
In finding your voice, you're not just discovering a way to speak up but uncovering the strength to live boldly in alignment with who you are created to be. Trust in your voice, knowing it is part of your God-given purpose.

One key element of reclaiming strength is understanding the power of perspective. When we shift our focus from what has happened to us to what can happen through us, we regain control over our narrative. Instead of seeing ourselves as victims of circumstance, we recognize our ability to shape our lives moving forward. The Bible offers many examples of individuals who, through God's strength, overcame their circumstances and walked in freedom. Joseph, for instance, endured betrayal and imprisonment, yet he declared, "You meant evil against me, but God meant it for good" (Genesis 50:20).

Each of us carries a unique journey filled with experiences that shape who we are. While the specifics of our stories may differ, one thing is certain: we all have a story to tell. You may not have walked through the same traumas or challenges that someone else has faced, but that doesn't mean your story is any less important or meaningful. It's easy to fall into the trap of thinking that because our pain, joy, or experiences aren't as visible or dramatic, they don't carry weight. Yet, in reality, every person's life is a testament to their journey, and every story is significant.

While the details of our stories may differ, the emotions behind them are often universal. Everyone experiences different forms of joy, sadness, triumph, loss, fear, love, and hope. Whether your story involves overcoming a major life challenge or navigating life's everyday ups and downs, the emotions and lessons are relatable.

For example, you may not have experienced trauma like abuse or loss, but perhaps you've dealt with other forms of hardship. Maybe you've struggled with self-doubt, experienced failure in a career pursuit, or navigated a difficult relationship. These experiences are valid, and they carry valuable lessons. Every person's story is a testament to their ability to navigate life's complexities. It's about surviving trauma and recognizing the growth and change that happen in everyday experiences.

I can't say that I am happy about anything I've experienced. I am grateful for the strength I've gained and the discovery of becoming who I am because of what I have endured. I would have never thought of all the women and girls I could reach and encourage from behind the chair. I have called behind the chair, for me, it was a pulpit, the place I loved, I cried with women, laughed, and even counseled.

Living in freedom is the opposite of living in fear. It's an attitude and a mindset recognizing that we are not bound by our circumstances, past mistakes, or other people's opinions. Freedom comes from understanding our worth in God's eyes and knowing that we are loved and valued unconditionally. Galatians 5:1 says, "It is for freedom that Christ has set us free. Stand firm, then, and do not let yourselves be burdened again by a yoke of slavery."

This freedom is not just about external liberty but internal release. It's freedom from the emotional and mental chains that keep us from stepping into our full potential. It's freedom from the fears that once dictated our actions and decisions. To live in freedom is to live with courage, trust in God's guidance, and have a mindset that recognizes that you are exactly where you need to be.

You are brave, resilient, and capable of standing tall in the face of adversity. You can reclaim your voice and strength no matter what you've been through. With confidence and boldness, you can step into the fullness of who you are meant to be. Your past does not define you, and fear has no place in your future. Stand firm in the knowledge that you are worthy, empowered, and unstoppable. You have everything within you to rise, speak your truth, and live boldly, knowing that you are stronger than any challenge you face.

Vernee Nycole

Owner Vernee Nycole House of Beauty

http://verneenycolehouseofbeauty.mysalononline.com/booking

Meet Vernee Nycole, a visionary in beauty and fashion. As the owner of Vernee Nycole House of Beauty, she's transformed countless clients with her innovative approach to hairstyling. Alongside her thriving salon, Vernee has launched a unique product line and clothing brand.

A published author and passionate speaker, Vernee empowers audiences on topics like self-care, entrepreneurship, and personal growth.

She also teaches aspiring beauty professionals, sharing her expertise in the industry. Don't miss her popular podcast, where Vernee dives into beauty trends and business strategies. Follow Vernee Nycole as she continues to inspire and lead.

Cutting Through Life

By: Vernee Nycole

Introduction
The salon chair is more than just a piece of furniture. It is a throne of transformation, a confession booth, a stage where countless stories are told. As a hairstylist, I have had the privilege of seeing the lives of my clients from a unique vantage point—behind the salon chair. Journey with me through some of the most memorable stories, lessons, and experiences I have gathered throughout my career. I hope you enjoy my colorful, emotional, and sometimes humorous world of hairstyling. Let me take you back to where it all began.

Discovering The Passion

The Early Days
I discovered my love for hair on a warm summer afternoon. My friends and I had been playing outside all day, jumping rope, and pretending to be teachers. As we settled on the porch to rest, I noticed my friend's hair, tangled and wild from playing all day. Without thinking, I grabbed a comb from the house and began to untangle her hair, French braiding it into what we thought was a cute style with beads.

The Porch Salon
Word quickly spread among my friends and parents, and soon, our porch turned into a salon. Each day we would play and run to the porch to play our favorite games. That porch was leanin', probably more than it should've been, with the paint chipped and the wood creaking under every step. The porch was alive with laughter, the smell of blue magic (hair grease), sulfur 8 and fresh-cut grass mixing with the warm summer air. You could hear the beads fall, clicking against the porch stairs, keeping time with our singing and storytelling. My hands moved through their hair like second nature, just braiding and chatting like we were our parents and their girlfriends. We'd be pulling at each other's hair, cracking jokes, sharing secrets, and just vibing as the sun dipped low, loving our

little salon in that golden-hour glow. It was here that my passion for hairstyling was born.

At the age of 8, my friends became my first clients. We would spend hours on the porch, playing games and styling hair. We would jump rope, play rock-teacher, and then settle down for a "hair appointment." Each head of hair was a new challenge, a new canvas for me to work on. The joy from my friends' faces after I styled their hair fueled my growing passion.

Learning and Experimenting
I started experimenting with unique styles and techniques. I would try out new braids, twists, and ponytails, learning what worked and what did not. My little friends were patient and supportive, always willing to let me practice on their hair. We laughed and kept playing when their hair beads would hit the ground. I just put them back in when we were done playing. Their trust and encouragement gave me the confidence to keep experimenting and improving.

Middle School Adventures

Expanding My Skills
As I entered middle school, my interest in hairstyling grew stronger. I would sit cross-legged on my bedroom floor, flipping through glossy pages of magazines, while sitting in front of the tv. My fingers traced the sleek, perfectly styled hairdos I saw. The smell of hairspray and flat irons filled the air as I practiced on my dolls, the sizzle of heat against hair sending wisps of steam into the room. With each twist and braid, my heart raced, excited by the thought of transforming ordinary hair into something extraordinary. If I saw someone at school or walking down the street with a style that I liked, I did it. I could figure out how to do any style I saw. Each new style I mastered felt like a small victory, a step closer to my dream of becoming a great stylist.

School Events and Special Occasions
I became the go-to stylist for school events and special occasions. Whether it was a birthday party, a school play, or just a regular day,

my friends would come to me for their hair needs. Their parents started sending them to ask me and pay as well. I was very shy; styling hair allowed me to express myself and connect with others. During these years, I began to see hairstyling as a paid hobby.

High School Dreams

The Reality of Career Choices
As I entered high school, my interest in hairstyling grew stronger. I became known for my creativity and natural gift for hair. Friends would often ask me to style their hair for special occasions. Despite my passion, I did not initially see hairstyling as a "real" profession. The societal pressure to pursue a more traditional and "honorable" career was strong. A professional career meant something more conventional, like becoming a doctor, lawyer, or engineer.

The Conversation with My Aunt
One day, my aunt, who had always been a strong influence in my life, asked me if I planned to work in a salon. Without hesitation, I replied, "No, I don't want to work in a salon. Maybe own my salon one day." It was a bold statement, one that surprised even me. At that moment, I realized that while I loved hairstyling, I also wanted to prove that it could be a respectable and successful career.

College and Realizations

Pursuing an "Honorable" Degree
After high school, I went away to college, driven by the desire to obtain what I believed was a more honorable degree. I chose a major that I thought would lead to a prestigious profession (psychology), Not realizing that the two go hand in hand. I spent countless hours in lectures, studying subjects that did not ignite my passion then. Deep down, I missed the joy and fulfillment of styling hair. I started doing hair in the dorms and my campus apartment. Seeing more money in exchange for hair styling changed my view of the profession.

The Moment of Clarity
During a particularly stressful class period, I had a moment of clarity. I went to the library and sat there, surrounded by textbooks,

feeling overwhelmed and disconnected. I realized that I was not pursuing my true passion. The memory of those carefree days on the porch styling my friends' hair flooded back. I missed the creativity, the connection, and the happiness that came with hairstyling.

Embracing the Dream

Changing Paths
After much contemplation, I left my traditional degree program and pursued my true passion. I remember the conversation with my mom like yesterday—the mass of excuses I built in response to the fear of failure. My mom said "where is your faith?" Do not you believe that GOD will provide everything you need to get through school? This shifted my perspective and reminded me of where my strength comes from. I decided to do it, afraid. I enrolled in cosmetology school, eager to learn everything I could about hairstyling. The transition was not easy, but I felt a sense of purpose and excitement that I had never experienced before.

The Support System
My family supported my decision wholeheartedly. They are the true witnesses of my anointing. My aunt reminded me of the confident young girl who boldly declared she would own her salon. My parents', family's, and clients' encouragement and belief in my dream gave me the strength to move forward. My friends and little cousins, who had been my first "clients," cheered me on, proud of my chosen path.

Building a Career

Starting in a Salon
Mark 6:4

A prophet is not without honor except in his own town, among his relatives and in his own home.

Although I had support and some success in my hometown of Chicago, it was not until I ventured beyond my familiar surroundings that my career began to blossom.

The House Call Phenomenon
One of my early clients became my unofficial promoter. She loved how I styled her hair and asked me to come to her house to do her hair regularly. Her home became my makeshift salon. I would set up in her kitchen on Saturdays, transforming it into a beauty hub.

It was not long before her friends and neighbors began showing up for appointments. They came individually, each bringing their own stories and hair challenges. The camaraderie and connection were unmatched. We laughed and shared life updates, and I became more than just their stylist—I became a confidante. Each new client brought more referrals, and soon, my days were fully booked with house calls.

I cherished these early days, driving across the city of Madison with my bag of tools, turning living rooms and kitchens into makeshift salons. It was exhausting but exhilarating. The connections I made, and the trust I earned were invaluable.

One afternoon, after I finished my very first client in Madison (Vicky), she handed me a business card. "How would you like to work in a salon?" she asked with a smile. I was surprised and curious, so I went to the interview. I began working in my first salon in Madison, "Style and Grace."

Working in the salon was a welcomed challenge, but it was also an incredible opportunity for growth. I learned so much from the experienced stylists around me, and I quickly realized this was where I was meant to be. The salon environment pushed me to refine my skills, expand my knowledge, and connect with diverse people. On Saturdays, I would set up in her kitchen with clients.

Each day brought new experiences and opportunities to learn. It was here that I learned how to get out of being shy. I was so used to listening to other people's stories that I learned to share my stories, too. My clientele grew steadily, and the word-of-mouth referrals from my house call days continued to bring in new clients. Before long, I had a loyal following.

Physical Transformations
One of the most exciting aspects of being a hairstylist is seeing the physical transformations. Whether it's an updo, a bold new color, or a fresh cut, the look on a client's face when they see themselves in the mirror is priceless. I remember one client at a time leaving the salon with a renewed sense of self. The confidence boost that comes with a fresh look can be life-changing.

Emotional Transformations
But it's not just about the physical changes. Hair has a powerful connection to our emotions and identities. I've had clients who were going through life-changing events—grief, breakups, losing jobs—come in for a haircut to take control and start fresh. Seeing the emotional transformation, the weight lifting off their shoulders, is incredibly rewarding.

I'll never forget the day Mrs. Chanice walked into the salon like she was carrying the weight of the world on her shoulders. Every step was slow, hesitant, and her eyes barely met mine as she sat down in the chair. There was a heaviness surrounding her, like she was trying to hold herself together but falling apart inside. It seemed to hurt to speak, just a quiet "Hey" as she tugged at her clothes, her hair covered with a scarf, like she hadn't really cared about herself in days. I could tell something was off.

I started with light conversation, trying to ease her into it, but she stayed quiet. As I began to shampoo her hair and started to work, I gently asked, "How've you been?" She was quiet for a moment, then her voice cracked as she whispered, "Honestly, not good at all." She looked down at her hands, avoiding the mirror. "I had a miscarriage," she said, her voice just above a whisper. "I feel like I failed... like I'm not enough."

My heart sank, but I didn't rush in with words. Instead, I paused and let her vent. I leaned in a little closer, my hands still working through her hair. "I'm so sorry for your loss," I said softly, "but you are enough. None of this is your fault." I could see the tears welling up in her eyes as she nodded, and we sat in that silence for a minute, allowing her the space to feel everything she needed to.

As I started blow drying her hair, I could feel her shoulders start to relax just a bit. The calming sound of the dryer—my hands moving through her hair—gave us both something to focus on. Slowly, she began to open up. She talked about how empty she felt, how it was hard to even look at herself the same as before in the mirror. "I just... I don't feel like myself anymore," she said quietly.

I began to start parting her hair, the fresh smell of clean hair filled the air. "I get that," I said. "But you're still you, even in this hard time. You don't have to be perfect or strong all the time. It's okay to not be okay."

She started to cry, but it wasn't the same kind of tears—there was release in them, like she was finally letting go of some of the weight she'd been carrying. By the time I finished her hair, there was a beautiful smile on her face. She caught her reflection in the mirror, and for the first time in days, she saw her eyes soften.

"You look beautiful," I said, and she looked back at me, this time with a little more light in her eyes. "Thank you," she whispered, touching her flawless hair, bouncing and behaving gently. "I feel... I don't know... I feel a little better." She paused. "Like I'm starting to find myself again, even if it's just a little bit."

We sat there for a while longer, no rush, just talking about life, about healing, and how sometimes the smallest acts of self-care—like getting your hair done—can remind you that you're still worthy of care and love, no matter what you've been through.

The Priceless Smile
It hit me, as I finished her silk press, what an honor it was for her to let me into such a vulnerable part of her life. Letting someone touch your hair isn't just about styling—it's about trust, especially when you're not feeling your best. She trusted me, trusted my hands to help her feel a little more like herself, even in the midst of struggle. I didn't take that lightly. I could feel the weight of that honor as I worked, knowing this wasn't just about a hairstyle.

When I handed her the mirror and she looked at herself, there was a quiet moment. The kind of moment where everything else just fades away. Her eyes softened, and that priceless smile began to brighten her face—slow at first, almost as if she wasn't sure it was okay to feel good. But then, it grew, and for a small second, the sadness that had been weighing her down seemed to lift.

"It's beautiful," she said, her voice a little stronger this time, touching the fresh press, as if she was reminding herself of who she was. I could see it in her eyes—that small spark of hope. It wasn't just the hair, it was that glimpse of herself again, the woman who still had so much strength even when she didn't feel like it.

Our Connection
We didn't need to say much after that. Sometimes the best encounters happen in the quiet, in the space between words. As she stood up, I could see that she was carrying herself just a little differently, like she'd found a bit of her old confidence again.

"I can't thank you enough," she said, looking at me with those tear-filled eyes that were no longer just full of grief and tears, but with gratitude, too. "You don't know how much this helped me today."

I smiled back at her. "You don't have to thank me. I'm just glad you let me be here with you for this divine appointment."

And as she left the salon, I reflected on how moments like these are why I do this—why I love what I do. It's more than just hair. It's about healing, connection, and the intentional ways we help each other through the toughest times. Her smile was priceless, yes, but even more so was the way she walked out of the salon with her head held a little higher, knowing she was enough—always had been, always will be.

Being a hairstylist requires a lot of patience and perseverance. There will be days when things don't go as planned, when the style doesn't come together as planned, or when a client is unhappy. It's important to stay consistent, learn from mistakes, and keep moving forward. Every challenge is an opportunity to grow and improve.

Conclusion

That business card from Vicky was the key that unlocked the next chapter of my career. It was a reminder that sometimes, the universe aligns in unexpected ways to guide us toward our true path. The transition from house calls to a professional salon was a pivotal moment in my journey, and it taught me the value of embracing every opportunity that comes my way.

As I look back on this time, I'm grateful for every client who trusted me, every challenge that pushed me to grow, and every small step that led me to where I am today. My journey as a hair

stylist is more than just a career—it's a testament to the power of passion, persistence, and the courage to follow your dreams even when you're scared.

The journey from a young girl braiding hair on the porch to a professional hair stylist has been filled with passion, creativity, and connection. The salon chair is more than just a place to get your hair done. It's a space of transformation, connection, and storytelling.

I hope that many stylists can see themselves in some way in my story. This book is giving you a glimpse into the world behind the salon chair and the incredible journey it took for me. Thank you for joining me on this adventure. But this is only the beginning. That business card from Vicky didn't just open the door to a new chapter; it set the stage for an even bigger dream—the dream of owning my own salon.

This is only the beginning of how I became the owner of the largest black Beauty/barber shop in Madison WI.

Regina McClarn

Founder Issa Slayy Boutique

www.Issaslayy.com
www.Trbeautybar.com
https://www.instagram.com/issaslayyboutique/

Regina McClarn is the passionate founder of Issa Slayy Boutique, a Madison, Wisconsin-based one-stop shop for natural beauty and fashion solutions. Inspired by her own childhood struggles, Regina established Issa Slayy Boutique to empower women by offering affordable, high-quality skincare, haircare, and fashion products. Each product is handcrafted with natural, gentle ingredients, reflecting her commitment to safety and holistic well-being.

As a mother of three boys and a devout woman of God, Regina skillfully balances family life with her entrepreneurial pursuits. She is dedicated to uplifting her community through her boutique and collaborative partnerships, such as with TR Beauty Bar and Boutique. Regina is a strong advocate for self-care, encouraging her customers to invest in their body, mind, and soul. Regina McClarn's story is one of resilience and empowerment, inspiring women to embrace their natural selves with confidence and grace.

Overcoming Darkness and Finding My Light

By: Regina McClarn

Introduction

Life can take us through some incredibly dark and challenging moments, times when the world seems devoid of hope and light. This chapter is dedicated to all the women who have faced such difficulties and challenges and yet found a way to rise above them, improving every day. This is my story, a testament to resilience, faith, and the power of healing.

Section 1: The Beginning of the Struggle

My journey into the depths of despair began with the heartbreaking loss of my children. Each loss felt like a piece of my soul was being torn away. The most devastating blow came when I was 17 weeks pregnant. I had just discovered that I was having another boy. Despite secretly wishing for a girl someday, I was filled with joy and anticipation at the thought of welcoming another son into the world. However, about a week later, complications arose. I was forced to give birth prematurely, and because my baby was too young to survive outside the womb, I had to endure the pain of giving birth and immediately losing him. This experience shattered me in ways I could never have imagined.

As I was 17 weeks, preparing to give birth, I knew in my heart that I wouldn't be able to take him home. The thoughts of not being able to change his diaper, give him his first bath, or breastfeed him consumed me. These thoughts weighed heavily on me even before the moment arrived. As the time to push came closer, I felt a wave of overwhelming sorrow. I wanted to cry more than I wanted to push because I knew that the faster I pushed, the sooner reality would hit me—I wasn't going to be able to keep him.

I was constantly pushing, trying to block out the emotional torment by covering my face. I didn't want my significant other to see me cry or witness the depth of my pain. The hardest part wasn't just pushing him out, but doing so while trying to hide the emotions that were tearing me apart inside. In that moment, I should have allowed myself to be vulnerable, to let him see me cry, to see how truly hurt I was.

Once I had pushed him out, I couldn't bring myself to look at him. The idea of holding my baby, knowing he wasn't going to take a breath, was too much to bear. The very thought of it turned my stomach. I couldn't physically or mentally prepare myself to look down at my son, knowing he wasn't alive. The pain was too intense, and I just couldn't do it.

The emotional and psychological toll of these losses was profound. I found myself questioning my worth as a woman and a mother. Society often teaches us that one of our primary roles is to bring life into the world. Failing to do so made me feel like I was failing at being a woman. My partner, who had children of his own, didn't face these issues, which only deepened my sense of inadequacy and insecurity.

Losing my baby at 17 weeks made it impossible for me to think clearly. I was lashing out at those around me, mainly my partner, who had nothing to do with my loss. It was hard to accept that I hadn't done anything wrong to deserve this pain. My mind was in turmoil, questioning everything, and it felt like if my baby was gone, my sanity might as well go too. This emotional chaos only deepened my sense of isolation and despair.

This grief infiltrated every aspect of my life. I struggled to be a good mother to my child. I couldn't find the strength or focus to run my business effectively. My financial situation spiraled out of control as I engaged in emotional spending sprees, trying to fill the void with material things that never brought the comfort I sought.

The dark space I was in extended beyond grief and insecurity. I found myself not wanting to exist in this world. There were times when I felt like I didn't want to be a mother, when the weight of my despair made it hard to get out of bed, to care for my child, to engage with the world around me. I felt defeated, lost, and utterly devoid of courage. I didn't feel beautiful as a woman because of my inability to have more children. Communication with my partner broke down as I isolated myself, unable to share the depth of my pain.

I was really having a hard time finding myself during this process. I remember I was doing eyelashes at one point, and boy, did I hate it doing those so bad, but it took me a while to recognize it. At another point, I was doing a job where I was collecting biohazard materials because it paid well. I stuck with it, not realizing that it wasn't something I really wanted. If I had been in a great headspace, I would have never taken that job, no matter how much it paid.

Section 2: The Turning Point

Amidst this darkness, a small glimmer of hope began to shine. I realized that I needed to seek help, to make a change, if I was ever going to find my way out. I turned to my faith, building a deeper connection with God. Prayer became my lifeline, a way to express my pain and seek comfort. This spiritual journey led me to the decision to get baptized, a symbolic act of cleansing and renewal.

But through the process of it all, I began to question why God would make me go through such things. I wondered if He truly loved me, why would He allow me to endure so much pain? Doubts flooded my mind, my soul, and my body. It was in this moment of questioning that I felt the deep need to turn my connection to God even deeper. I sought to understand His plan for me and to make sense of everything that had happened. Turning to God was a necessary step in my healing journey. It allowed me to see things from a different perspective, to find a sense of peace, and to trust that there was a purpose behind the pain.

Recognizing the need for professional help, I sought therapy. Admitting that I needed help was a significant step, one that allowed me to start addressing my mental health. Therapy provided a space where I could process my grief and begin to heal. It was okay to be vulnerable, to admit that I was struggling, and to seek the support I desperately needed.

Section 3: The Path to Healing

My path to healing was gradual and required continuous effort. I maintained a consistent prayer life, which strengthened my faith and provided solace. Therapy helped me unpack the layers of grief and pain, allowing me to rebuild my emotional strength. I also leaned on my loved ones, embracing the support and encouragement they offered.

As I began to heal, I noticed positive changes in my life. My relationship with my child improved as I became more present and engaged. My business started to recover as I regained my focus and determination. Slowly but surely, I was emerging from the darkness.

Section 4: Rebuilding and Rediscovering Myself

As I continued on my healing journey, I realized the importance of working on myself. I needed to focus on becoming a better person before I could be a better mother or partner. This period of self-discovery and growth was crucial. I learned to prioritize my well-being, setting boundaries, and making time for self-care.

Issa Slayy Boutique became a significant part of this process. My boutique is a one-stop shop for all-natural hair and skincare products. It's a space where I can pour my creativity and passion, providing others with the tools to enhance their beauty naturally. Working on my business gave me a sense of purpose and direction. It was more than just a job; it was a part of my healing journey.

In addition to Issa Slayy Boutique, I founded TR Beauty Bar and Boutique, another one-stop shop for all beauty needs, including clothing and other necessities. These businesses not only helped me regain my confidence but also allowed me to inspire and support other women. They became platforms for empowerment, demonstrating that it's possible to overcome adversity and build something beautiful out of pain.

Section 5: Embracing Honesty and Vulnerability

One of the most important lessons I learned during this journey was the power of honesty and vulnerability. I had to be honest with myself and those around me about why I was struggling, why I was withdrawing, and why I needed help. Admitting my struggles was not a sign of weakness, but of strength. It allowed me to reconnect with my loved ones and rebuild those relationships.

Picking up the pieces and addressing the things I had left unfinished was challenging but necessary. It was part of my commitment to becoming a better person, for myself and for those around me. I realized that it was okay to ask for help, to lean on others, and to take the time I needed to heal.

Conclusion: Finding Light and Moving Forward

Through faith, therapy, and the support of my loved ones, I found my way out of the darkness. I embraced the idea that it's okay to take time to heal, to be transparent in moments of vulnerability, and to seek help when needed. My businesses, Issa Slayy Boutique and TR Beauty Bar and Boutique, became extensions of my healing journey, helping me to regain my confidence and purpose.

Today, I am proud to say that I have won awards and received nominations for my work. I have two thriving businesses that not only provide for my family but also inspire and empower others. None of this would have been possible without the resilience, faith, and support that carried me through the darkest times.

This chapter is a testament to the strength that lies within us all. No matter how deep the darkness, there is always a way to find the light. We must be willing to seek help, embrace vulnerability, and have faith that better days are ahead.

What's Your Next Step?

The stories in *Healing Voices: From Behind the Chair* offer more than inspiration—they serve as a reminder that transformation is within reach for each of us. Now, it's time to reflect on your own journey!

Whether you're seeking personal growth, deeper connections, or a renewed sense of purpose, this book is just the beginning. We encourage you to embrace your story, share your voice, and continue to explore the power of vulnerability and connection.

Here's how you can continue this journey:

1. Reflect and Share: Journal your thoughts as you read. What resonates with you? How can you apply the lessons of resilience and connection in your own life? Share your reflections on social media using the hashtag #HealingVoices to join the conversation.

2. Connect with the Authors: The women featured in this anthology are more than storytellers; they are leaders in their fields. Follow their journeys, explore their work, and find out how their expertise can support your own path. Visit our website https://www.healingvoicesfrom.com/ to learn more about Aundrea and the authors.

3. Join the Movement: We believe in the power of shared healing. Become a part of our community where we continue these conversations. Sign up for our newsletter for exclusive content, upcoming events, and opportunities to engage with other like-minded individuals who are also on a journey of transformation.

Your story matters. Embrace your path, and know that, like the women in this book, you have the strength to inspire and create change. Let's continue to uplift, empower, and transform together.

For partnership or collaboration opportunities email
aundreabooker@gmail.com

Milton Keynes UK
Ingram Content Group UK Ltd.
UKHW021457011224
451693UK00013B/1264